Brooke Blurton is a proud Noongar-Yamatji woman and a passionate mental health advocate and champion of young people, especially First Nations and queer youth, and all people of colour. Brooke developed her passion for mental health advocacy as a youth worker by reflecting on her own challenging journey, and by educating young people about essential life skills, including Aboriginal Mental Health First Aid. Brooke was a contestant on the 2018 season of Network Ten's *The Bachelor* and the 2019 season of *Bachelor in Paradise*, and she starred as the first Indigenous and bisexual suitor on the 2021 season of *The Bachelorette*. Brooke is an RUOK Ambassador, supports the Uluru Statement from the Heart via the Uluru Youth Network, and is a champion for LGBTIQ groups. She lives in Naarm (Melbourne).

BIG LOVE

BIG LOVE

Brooke Blurton

*Reclaiming myself,
my people,
my country*

HarperCollins*Publishers*

CONTENT WARNINGS

Aboriginal and Torres Strait Islander people should be aware that *Big Love* contains descriptions, images and names of people now deceased.

Big Love contains descriptions that may be confronting or disturbing for some readers, including references to death, suicide and suicide attempts, substance abuse and overdoses, violence, abuse, childhood trauma, sexual assault, homelessness, mental illness and mental distress. Please be mindful of these and other possible triggers and seek assistance if needed from the resources at the end of the book.

HarperCollins*Publishers*
Australia • Brazil • Canada • France • Germany • Holland • India
Italy • Japan • Mexico • New Zealand • Poland • Spain • Sweden
Switzerland • United Kingdom • United States of America

HarperCollins acknowledges the Traditional Custodians
of the land upon which we live and work, and pays respect
to Elders past and present.

First published in Australia in 2022
by HarperCollins*Publishers* Australia Pty Limited
Gadigal Country
Level 13, 201 Elizabeth Street, Sydney NSW 2000
ABN 36 009 913 517
harpercollins.com.au

A catalogue record for this book is available from the National Library of Australia

ISBN 978 1 4607 6151 9 (paperback)
ISBN 978 1 4607 1453 9 (ebook)
ISBN 978 1 4607 4552 6 (audiobook)

Cover and internal design by Mietta Yans, HarperCollins Design Studio
Cover photograph by Jarrad Seng
Original artwork, *Mob and Family*, by Brooke Blurton, 2020
Typeset in Bembo Std by Kirby Jones
Printed and bound in Australia by McPherson's Printing Group

MIX
Paper | Supporting
responsible forestry
FSC® C001695
www.fsc.org

This book was written on the traditional lands of the Wurunjeri people of the Kulin nation, and on the traditional lands of the Noongar people living on Whadjuk Noongar Boodjar.

The author acknowledges the Traditional Owners and Custodians of the lands on which she works, and pays respects to Elders past and present. Sovereignty has never been ceded. It was and always will be Aboriginal land.

The author supports the Uluru Statement from the Heart to achieve justice, recognition, and respect for First Nations people and a referendum to enshrine a First Nations Voice in the Constitution.

For Charlotte, Seanna,
Kyandra, Eden, Troy and RJ

Prologue

I'd be lying if I said I wasn't emotional. Standing here on the red carpet, in front of three Elders from the Darug nation, witnessing the first ever Welcome to Country performed to open a season of *The Bachelorette*, the tears coming from my eyes are genuine.

I've never been able to fake it, anyway. Everything I feel is always clear to anyone around me – it's just how I am.

But this moment is so much bigger than I anticipated. It's not my first rodeo – I've been on this carpet before, and it's difficult to think back to that younger Brooke without feeling a pang of heartbreak for her. At twenty-three, I had no idea what a rollercoaster I was stepping onto as a contestant on Season Six of *The Bachelor*.

I remember walking up the red carpet to meet Nick Cummins, the suitor, two footballs tucked under my arm while I tried to navigate high heels and a fancy dress, my heart full of hope and excitement. I thought I'd already given everything I could to television when I left that season, heartbroken and still single.

But here I am, back again. I guess you could call me a hopeless romantic.

In this moment, listening to Uncle Colin Locke welcome us to country alongside Uncle Peter Williams and Uncle Wayne

Cornish, I'm reminded that this season of *The Bachelorette*, its seventh, is about so much more than my own quest for love. It's about representation. It's about community, and claiming a space for my people.

As the first Aboriginal Bachelorette, I'm making my own mark on history. I'm taking a step forward for my people by showing that we can and we should take up space everywhere in Australia, including on one of the biggest spots on free-to-air television, as the Bachelorette.

I've spent my entire life fighting the stereotypes and misconceptions about Aboriginal and Torres Strait Islander people, which have been our cross to bear since invasion. To be standing here now as a hero in my own story, knowing that this Welcome to Country will be screened to hundreds of thousands of Australians across the country, I am filled with pride.

'You can't be it if you can't see it,' Osher says in his introduction. And it's so true. Growing up, I never saw anyone like me in the public eye. I had to use all of my imagination to dream big dreams for myself. I think of the little girls who might watch me when this season airs, who might feel just a little less alone seeing someone like me on their screens, and I feel the certainty again that I've made the right decision by coming back on the show.

I haven't taken this decision lightly. I've had my heart broken twice on national television, and it hasn't been easy to bounce back. The last two years, off screen, have been big ones. I have loved again, and I have lost again, but I have also healed.

I'm ready to find the person I can share the rest of my life with.

And although it's my third time in front of the cameras, it's my first time being here completely and authentically as myself – a proud Noongar-Yamatji woman, and also a proud and open bisexual woman. I will be the first queer Bachelorette, and I can't exaggerate how privileged I feel to be able to take this step forward for the LGBTQIA+ community.

I think about the years I spent trying to fit into a heterosexual identity – the love I gave up and denied myself because I was afraid to confront the truth of my sexuality – and how much of a relief it was to claim my true identity. I think about how hard that might be for young people today battling with the same questions I have, and I know that this is and will be a historic moment. I feel so honoured to be given this chance to represent the communities I belong to. But I'm also not taking the responsibility lightly. I'm nervous. I try not to fidget on the carpet, to push my nerves aside.

I hug the Elders who have welcomed me to country, and they give me strength in that moment. Now we're waiting for the first contestant's limo to pull up.

The sky is blue-black above me, and I suddenly feel a long way from home.

My country is Noongar and Yamatji in Western Australia, on the other side of the continent. Right now, I am so, so far away. I can feel that tug, calling me back to country. My mother and my nan are both tethering me to home, their bodies buried in the soil of our ancestors.

People who watch this season will see one side of me, a young woman well used to the camera, gliding across their screens, wearing beautiful clothes, meeting beautiful people, living a sort of dream life. But they don't know where I've come from. They don't know just how high the odds were stacked against my survival, let alone my arrival on this red carpet as the first Aboriginal, bisexual Bachelorette.

I have survived so much to be here – racism, poverty, sexual assault, the loss of my mother and my nan when I was so young, the separation of my family, the deterioration of my own mental health, and too many heartbreaks for me to count. I have overcome all of these adversities, and somehow I've kept a small spark of hope alive inside me, which has led me to be here now, a woman in a black dress with an open heart, waiting to find love.

I can hear the sound of a car now, and my heart is thudding again. I take a deep breath, and let it out gently, grounding myself in the moment. I look up at the sky, and set my intention.

This is for you, Mum and Nan, I think, calling on the two strongest women I have known, who have made me who I am today. Whatever happens now, I will stand in my truth and take it in my stride.

Love has guided me here, and love will be with me, no matter what happens next.

The limo pulls up. I can hear my heart beat as if there's a microphone at my chest. The door opens. It begins.

One

Every story starts somewhere, and parts of mine have been told by a lot of others so far. So this is me taking it back. This time, it's just me and you here – no camera, no make-up, no screens. The real Brooke, barefoot and uncomplicated, with my whole truth to share.

It starts long before anyone knew my name, other than the mob and family who loved me and knew me from the day I was born.

Compared to others, my childhood was an unusual one. There are two stories that I could tell about it. One could be about all the things we didn't have, like food in the fridge, clean beds to sleep in every night, stability and the routine of breakfast, school, homework and dinner that most kids take for granted.

But that wouldn't be a true story, because that isn't what has made me who I am. It isn't what took me from a girl with very little to a woman with power, passion and skills to give to her community. The other story – the true story – about what has made me who I am is the one thing that I never went without. Love. Big love, which filled me up and made me feel like there was a future for me. The kind of love that's unconditional, and that lasts across time, space, and even death.

My family was poor, but we loved each other. My mum, Seanna, was an addict, but she loved us to the best of her ability. My nan, Charlotte, my mum's mum, was stretched – her whole life was full of hardship, but she was fierce with her love. As were my three brothers, and my sister – despite all the trauma they endured and the lifelong difficulties that came with that, they never once made me question their love.

Along the way, there has also been the love of my mob, especially my aunties, uncles and cousins, who showed up for me through the good times and bad, who understood who I was and where I came from. And the love of strangers, like my teacher and guardian Jo, who took me in and gave me a chance when there was nowhere for me to go as a teenager. The girls I played football with, who gave me a community and a safe space to figure myself out, to discover my sexual identity and my true self. The people I met through *The Bachelor* and *The Bachelorette*, from both in front of and behind the camera, who have become lifelong friends, who gave me so much more from the experience of television than what viewers can ever see. The communities I've grown and become part of online and offline, the queer communities that have embraced me for who I am, with no filters.

And the men and women who I have loved, deeply, truly and with all of my heart and soul. Even when the relationship hasn't lasted, the love has been real and will be part of my life forever.

This story is about love. But it's an unconventional story, and I know there will be readers who'll be confronted by what I share in this book. Poverty is messy and ugly, just like addiction and family violence and suicide and mental illness, and the intergenerational trauma that all mob have as a result of white colonisation, which has reverberated painfully through our people for more than 230 years.

So I know this isn't an easy thing to understand, but I ask that you read my story with the openness and love that I am bringing to the telling of it.

I grew up in Western Australia. The country of my people, the Noongar, is one made of wide expanses: of sky, sand, sea, scrub. This is my grandmother's country – Ballardong country. The other country I lay claim to is the land of the Yamatji people, which is my birthplace and where my mum grew up.

These landscapes are as much a part of me as my people are a part of them. You could say I was forged right out of the Yamatji waters – because I was, literally! When Mum was pregnant with me she would swim in the turquoise waters at the Bluff near Quobba Station, a dusty drive away from where we lived in Carnarvon, and on one very special afternoon, there were sea turtles popping up all around her. I like to think they came to welcome me, a child of the water, just like my mum. We're connected to the sea, and my totem is a sea turtle. I still feel the most calm, the most collected, when I'm in the ocean, connected to my country.

Most of my childhood was spent between Carnarvon, on the north coast of Western Australia, Perth, and Quairading, which is a couple of hours east of Perth – my nan's country and her home. Maybe there were other places in between. It's hard for me to know, because my memory of my early childhood is pretty sticky. I can catch glimpses of it out of the corner of my eye, but it's hard to look at it straight on.

My mental health training knows that it's trauma that does this to our memories; our body's defense mechanism protecting us from the things it knows will hurt. But some memories have stuck, and I can remember specific moments so vividly that I could be right back there with that little girl, living each moment in the chaos of her surrounds. But even when things were messy around me, I always knew who I was. I can remember that about myself, even as a kid.

One of my earliest memories is of a school day morning. I am small, little even as a child, and old enough for early primary school. I'm kneeling on the floor of our house in Neerabup, an outer suburb of Perth, and it's early, the others not up just yet.

I have my school skirt with me. It's the classic Aussie uniform skirt, the kind that all primary school girls wore in the early 2000s. It has a zip, and pleats, and it's made from scratchy nylon, and designed to last a long time, not for comfort.

The skirt might not be completely clean, but I'm sitting on the floor with an iron plugged into the wall next to me, and I'm trying to iron the pleats straight in the skirt. I probably shouldn't have been anywhere near a hot iron; it would have weighed almost as much as I did, I was so small. But no one else was going to iron my skirt and I wanted it to look like my fellow classmates'.

This memory of myself as a tiny little girl with the innocent mind of a child, trying to fix just one thing about myself to fit in better at school, breaks my heart.

Even then, I knew that it mattered what impression I gave. The other kids all seemed as if they had warm and safe homes with parents who washed and ironed their school uniforms and packed their lunches, the same parents who kissed the tops of their heads when they dropped them at the school gates. Those kids were 'normal', and I knew that my life wasn't. I knew how hard life could be when you were different like me.

It wasn't just my crumpled uniform that stood out. My skin was darker than other kids', my mum wasn't like theirs, and my house definitely didn't look like theirs. I tried to iron those pleats into my skirt to mask at least some of that difference, because as a kid I hadn't learned yet that difference could be something to celebrate, instead of something to hide. And it would be a long while before that happened.

Love looked different in our house, too. All of us kids – Kyandra, Eden, me, Troy and Ronald Jerome – grew up fast, me especially. It made me self-sufficient, grounded in who I am and with a strong sense of resourcefulness. I've been hustling since I was a kid, and the independence that came with that is something I'll never shake.

Mum had five kids, and we were split into two groups by age. My sister Kyandra – or Ky as we called her – came first, and then my brother Eden after her. As they were just that bit older than the rest of us, Ky and Eden were out of the house more and to me they didn't feel like 'kids' when I was growing up.

Of the five of us, I was smack in the middle – maybe, like a lot of middle children, I was the easiest to forget or skip over, not one of the teens getting in trouble and not one of the younger kids needing looking after. I reckon it's what made me the mother hen that I turned into, always looking after my two younger brothers, Troy, and Ronald Jerome, RJ for short.

We all have different fathers, and they have played different roles in each of our lives over the years. I would stay with my own dad off and on as a kid, but the majority of my childhood was spent with Mum, Nan and my brothers and sister.

Ky was really independent from a young age. She left school when she was only eleven or twelve, and I remember her using drugs from a young age too. My early childhood memories of her are patchy, but she always seemed to be coming and going, in and out of the house with her friends and boyfriends.

Eden and I hung out a lot when we were kids, especially when Troy was still really little. Eden is about four years older than me, and I remember him as a cheeky-faced kid with rich, dark skin, white teeth and a wild mop of hair. He was always grinning then, and we got up to some real trouble together. When he started high school, Eden went to live with Grandma Susette for a few years – Susette was a family friend from Perth – and the next time I saw him, that happy-go-lucky kid had become a quiet teenager, though he wasn't exactly quiet when he was blasting Metallica out of his bedroom!

Troy and I were the closest in some ways – he's about four years younger than me, and I was mothering him from the day he was born. I can remember changing his nappy on the floor of our house in Neerabup, only four or five years old myself. I have no idea how I knew how to change a nappy at that age, but I have a photo of us, probably just after one of these sessions, and I look proud, my little brother sitting there with a babyish look of surprise on his face.

RJ, the youngest, has the least memories of us all being together, because he was only three when Mum died. I've always felt a sort of guilt for not seeing him more, when he went to live with his dad, Dragan. But we're close now – all of my brothers and I – and I'm grateful every day that we've stayed connected as a family, even with all the chaos that we've been through.

Some of my strongest memories are from Carnarvon, in the three-bedroom housing commission house that we lived in on and off over for years. There could be up to nine of us living in the house – us kids, Mum and her partner, and Nan, and often my Uncle Ronald. Troy and I slept with Nan, and I loved being able to snuggle against her and fall asleep with her telling us stories.

Charlotte Rose Blurton, my nan, was a six feet tall, fierce woman. True as God, she was the best storyteller you ever came across – her stories could go for hours, and no one ever interrupted because they were such good yarns.

She'd talk about her arthritis from all the basketball she used to play when she was younger, often rubbing Goanna Oil liniment into her joints and making it known what a deadly player she was back in her day. I'd sit on the floor in front of her for hours, massaging her calves, and she'd be yarning, telling us kids about what she got up to with her brothers and sisters. She was one of twelve, so there were loads of stories. Her parents, Gladys and John Blurton, raised their brood out on Ballardong country in towns like Quairading, Beverley, and York. New Norcia Mission was a well-known place for them, too. It was an institution for Aboriginal children, run by the Catholic Church – many of these children had been removed from their families, and it was also the site of a lot of suffering at the hands of the monks and nuns there.

Even though she loved to yarn, Nanna would barely talk about that mission. She said she didn't remember it much, but I know she did. Nanna was a very subtle, very confident, but calm woman. She didn't talk about those days on the mission because she didn't want to think about them – I get that now. But as a kid, I just loved listening to Nanna no matter what she was talking about.

She was like my hero, my protector. When she stood behind me, I felt as if I had my own bodyguard, like a celebrity. Because no matter what, she always made me feel as though I was the most important person in the room to her.

One of the things that makes me sad, especially as I tell this story, is that so much of the life we shared as a family is only left to our memories. We didn't have the luxuries of cameras to take photos with, and I've only got a handful – just enough to capture the haircuts and fashion choices I made as a teen, and some even more precious: photographs of Mum and Nan, and all us kids. These ones are so special they're like sacred relics, and I've made sure to save them all as digital copies so there's no danger of ever losing them.

But I still have the ring and watch that Nan was wearing when she passed away. I treasure those, because they keep me connected to her, and they've reminded me over the years that if I ever had the chance, I would record our lives and our story, because I never want hers, or ours, to be forgotten.

Nan did her best for us, her grandchildren. She gave us as much stability as she could. She was only a teenager when she had her own first child. Our grandfather was a Malaysian man, and I think that's where Mum, Ky and I got our petite frames from. He and Nan split before I was born.

In my early life, there was Nan, and then there was Mum – my two guardian angels. My story is as much my mum's story, because I am so much a product of her.

Her name was Seanna, spelled S E A, as in ocean. She loved the salt water; it was her favourite place, and whenever she was close to it, she was at peace. She was a courageous woman who showed maturity beyond her years, as if she'd walked this earth before.

Mum was a beauty. She'd walk into a room and you could hear a pin drop. She had long, thick, jet black hair that swung all the way down her back to her bum, and she had this swagger that just oozed out of her. Her power would draw you in, but there was also a side to her that made you feel a little scared of her. She was fierce.

Mum was the baby of Charlotte's five children, all from different fathers. Mum had two brothers on her dad's side, too, after he remarried. Even though Seanna was the youngest, in a lot of ways she had the most expectation weighing on her. It's always been like that in our family, a little like how I'm the 'eldest' in my family, even if I'm not in age. My uncles and aunties have been a big part of my life – Uncle Derek, Uncle Murray (who died young), Aunty Coral, and Uncle Ronald – or as we called him, 'Uncle Pinhead', because he had a small head, apparently!

In Carnarvon and Perth, like most mob, our family extended way beyond blood relatives to the close community around us. In our culture, it doesn't matter if you're related by blood or not – we're all family to each other, and the relationships we share are generational. So the older women and men who were Nan's generation were all Nannas and Pops, the women and men of Mum's generation were Aunties and Uncles, and the kids I grew up with, in the houses up and down our street, were my brothers and sisters and cousins.

It's hard sometimes trying to explain this to people who aren't First Nations, because there's an expectation that I pin down exactly where and how our family tree maps to each relation. It's a very Western idea of family and community, and it doesn't fit with the way we connect beyond blood, through culture and country. It doesn't fit with the way colonisation and intergenerational trauma made us closer as a community out of a need to preserve what's left of our culture.

For Mum, I know that a really important part of her youth was with the girls she grew up with in Carnarvon, especially Aunty Katrina and Aunty Ricki, both First Nations women who lived down the road from her. They were like sisters, and both Aunties have been a big part of my life, too.

I don't know a lot about what Mum's life was like when she was growing up or before she had kids, but I can gauge what she was like from the stories I've been told. She would have moved around a lot, like we did, because I know she spent time in Carnarvon and Perth over the years of her childhood and adolescence.

People who knew Seanna compare me to her quite a bit; they say that I have her determination and her perseverance. They also say I have a mouth like she had, meaning I can talk the talk!

One of the best insights I have into what Mum was like is from a letter of hers, which she wrote when she was about twelve. It was to one of her friends, Rachel, who'd moved away from Carnarvon. Reading it, you can tell Mum was full of spark, and was clearly bossy. She wrote (with punctuation added):

Dear Rachel,
How are you? Just to let you know I'm fine. Could you please
say hello to Ronald Robert and family and friends. Well,
anything happening lately? As you should know this town has
been dead and boring since all youse left. I've been in a little
trouble lately – I've been wagging school for the first time, nearly
for a week. At the time I thought it was fun – mind you, don't let
me hear that you've been wagging school 'cause I tell ya, it's not

*worth it, cause I've never ever seen a brainy Aborigine who isn't
at school, so now I've got myself a lot of homework to do to catch
up for the four days I haven't been. I hope you enjoy my photos —
after all I'm beautiful, don't you think? Nah, I'm just joking,
or don't you think so? Well, that doesn't matter now, what does
matter is that I have to catch up on the homework I didn't do.*

You can tell she was a bit of a jokester, she didn't take herself too
seriously, and she was determined to do her homework! I can see
a bit of me in this letter too — always up for a laugh, but secretly
also wanting to do the right thing.

One thing I've been told is that Mum loved being around
kids. You'd often find her walking around with one on her hip,
perhaps a cousin's or friend's child; there was always a baby to be
found. She was also always bossing whichever older kids were
around, rallying them to jump onto the bus that would take them
to the PCYC – the Police and Community Youth Services club –
in Carnarvon, one of the only places in our small town where
kids got access to organised activities and games. There was a
rollerdrome and a youth centre, even a regular Blue Light Disco.

My Uncle Pete, who has become like a dad to me, was in
his twenties when Mum, Aunty Ricki and Aunty Katrina were
teenagers. Pete was an optometrist and ran a clinic in Carnarvon,
and he also used to drive the PCYC bus. He remembers Mum
and Katrina and Ricki being cheeky ringleaders at the time.

Uncle Pete tracked me down years later, because he was
thinking about Seanna, and Aunty Brenda, another member of
our sprawling mob, had given him my number. We caught up,
and he's given me so many precious memories of Mum when
she was younger. Since then we've stayed close, and he's been a

source of so much comfort to me. He's a link to Mum as well, at a more carefree time in her life before it was defined by drugs and the challenges of her mental health.

Pete told me that he first met Mum when Nan brought her in as a teenager to his optometry clinic. 'Charlotte came in because Seanna was getting headaches, and it was making it hard for her to do her schoolwork,' he told me. 'Charlotte wanted Seanna to have the opportunity to learn; it was something her father wanted for her, too.'

Pete was very community minded, and he wanted to help his younger patients with their education beyond their eyesight. He offered to tutor Mum, and he would come by their house in the afternoons after school and help her study. He remembered one afternoon in particular – they were doing maths homework – when Mum said, 'I like numbers. You can rely on them. People … ' and she trailed off. I think about that sometimes – even as a young teen, Mum was worldly and she knew that people could and would let her down.

But for the most part, her childhood and adolescence sound like they were full of good times, despite the hardships of being poor. Pete told me that, as Carnarvon was a small country town, the whole community was close, that they'd all spend time at the beach together, or drive out to the blowholes near Quobba Station, and snorkel and hang out at the Bluff. It sounds idyllic, and not that different to some of the best times in my own childhood.

It's hard to think of Mum back then, though, because I can picture her as an innocent young person, still full of potential and optimism. It aches, because I know what her life turned into, and it didn't include her reaching that potential, unfortunately.

I only ever knew Mum as an addict. Sometimes, I wonder what she was like underneath it all, or if things had turned out differently. If she'd been born into a family that was stable, without the poverty and hardships that Nan had raising her children, would Mum have made different choices? Would she have stayed with us for longer? My whole life, I've felt an urgent push to live up to my potential, because Mum never got to do that. I want to do it for both of us.

I've always been a bit spiritual, and on some level, I've always felt as if the universe has had a plan for me. I was born at 5.56 am at Carnarvon Hospital on the first day of January in 1995 – born into the early breaths of a new year, as if I were put here to start something.

Mum named me Brooke, short for 'Brooklyn'. Apparently Mum and Dad fought about this, because Dad wanted me to be named Brooke for his favourite character in the old soap opera *Days of Our Lives*, but Mum loved the idea of Brooklyn, the famous borough of New York. He won in the end, and Mum gave me the middle name Ashley, after her midwife. (I often feel the urge to track down this woman who made such a big impression on Mum!)

Thinking about my early life, I would describe it as 'unconventional', with a side of 'dysfunctional', and very far from 'normal'. There are so many things that felt normal to me, things that will sound pretty crazy to anyone who's had a more conventional life. But I'll try my best to explain it in all of its messy glory.

For us and for mob in general, family means everything. We always had our own struggles, but through it all we looked out for each other. In Carnarvon, having our aunties and uncles and cousins living next door and in the streets around us meant that us kids always had a safe place to land – even if that place looked a little chaotic from the outside.

I remember big parties in the backyards of the houses on the street. The adults would light a fire to gather around, and there would be loads of food, something that was very rare for us, because we were used to going hungry. Us kids would grab all the food we could snag and watch TV on the floor of the lounge room, with doonas and pillows from wherever we could find them. Sometimes we'd fall asleep there in one big group, and be woken up later when, inevitably, one of the adults would start an argument or a fight. If things were rowdy, one of our aunties would come and nudge us awake, and take us back to another house, away from the party, where we could sleep and dream in peace.

My Aunty Ricki lived next door to us, and like all the other women in my extended family, she was a matriarch. A strong, proud blak woman who carried the weight of her family on her shoulders, and still somehow managed to find the time and energy to give that little bit extra to anyone who needed it.

Aunty Ricki would send her kids, my cousins, over in the morning to collect me and Troy so we could walk to school together. I would get Troy up, who was bleary-eyed and reluctant, and some days I would climb up on a chair in front of the stove and make porridge. Oats and water, and sugar if we had any. I remember one day pouring in what I thought was sugar, only to discover that it was salt, and watching my brother spit bits of the bitter meal out, laughing and shouting.

Once we were fed and dressed, we'd start the walk to school with our cousins. When you're a kid, you don't always realise how your life compares to everyone else's. But I always knew we were different. It was there in the way teachers looked at us sometimes, and in the way they shifted uncomfortably when they saw our skinny limbs and hungry eyes.

Outside of school, in town, it was even more clear. I can't say when I knew it, but there was a knowledge deep in my bones that there were things that white people could do that we just couldn't get away with, like being rowdy in a shop. When we entered the supermarket or shopping centre, eyes narrowed. People were on guard, security officers clocked us straight away. Just the colour of our skin, the sound of our voices, was enough to set suspicions rising.

I can remember noticing the way adults spoke to my mum, and realising that she didn't hold any respect in their eyes. She was an addict, and she was Indigenous, and that was sometimes all anyone saw when they looked at her. People talked down to her with impatience and aggression at times, as though everything about her was offensive to them. I hated seeing her treated that way. I knew what it meant to feel shame before I ever knew there was a word for it.

Some days after school I'd go to my friends' houses, and it was like a glimpse into a life that I knew existed, but was still amazed by. They had carpets that had been vacuumed, and walls that were clean. There was food in the fridge – so much food! Fruit bowls on counter tops, cereal in the cupboard, luxuries I couldn't even comprehend. My stomach would ache just looking at the packets of biscuits, and the sliced cheese and bread just waiting to be slapped together and scoffed down.

My fingers would itch, dying to grab as much as I could and shove it in my mouth, but my manners were still impeccable, instilled in me by Nan, and I would wait for it to be offered. Sitting with friends in front of the TV, those few blissful hours were like a little holiday from my life. As they went through the comforting routine of bath, then dinner and bed, I'd be wandering home to see if there was anything for dinner, or if it would be another night of scrounging around for whatever we could find.

Back home, things always looked a little different after a few hours in another world. I could see it all the more clearly. Our house, a housing commission property that we loved, which felt like ours even though we could have lost it at any time, was a wreck. There were holes in the walls, kicked or punched in during a party or a fight. There was always stuff all over the floor – clothes, rubbish, debris, empty food containers; whatever had been dropped by someone on the way to do something else.

Our clothes would be thrown into the washing machine during one of Mum's sober moments, a brief interlude when she had the energy to think about housework or laundry. But then they would sit there, sopping wet and neglected, until they got mouldy and smelly, and had to be salvaged from the machine by one of us.

Sometimes, after visiting a friend's house after school, I would come home and look at the mess and want to do something. I wanted to make our house like the ones I had been in. As a child, I could only see our differences, not the reasons for them. So I would sweep all the rubbish on the floor into piles, using just a dustpan brush. We had no pan, so I would find bits of paper or cardboard and use that to scoop up the rubbish, and take it to the bin. The floor was still dirty, dust and grime having been trodden in over time, but in those moments, for a brief flash, I could see how our house could be like everyone else's. Then life would happen again, and within hours the floor would be returned to its previous state.

Poverty isn't something you can brush away, and our mess was the same as poor families across Australia. Cleaning is a luxury. It might not seem like one, not when you've never had to toss up whether to buy dishwashing liquid or bread for a dollar, or when you haven't had to struggle to make it through a single day battling through the fog of depression. Or the time spent trying to figure out how to keep everyone fed and clothed for another day takes it out of you so much that all you want to do is lie down with a bevvy and a moment of silence.

Something that seems as simple as cleaning is a luxury. The older I get and the more I experience, I've realised that the majority of Australians talk about life as if we are all given a fair set of choices, and what we end up with is the result of those choices. But some choices are made with a freedom that others simply don't have.

There are choices I made as a kid that I look back on now and feel my heart ache, remembering the immediacy of my needs and how rarely they were fulfilled. I have a memory of one of the houses we lived in, in Neerabup; this is in the years before we moved to Carnarvon. I must have been five or six, and like all of my memories, these ones are somewhat patchy. But some are crystal clear in my mind.

The house was another social housing property, and like all of the flats and units and houses we lived in over the years – even women's refuges or shelters when things were really desperate we knew that it had been the site of many other families' struggles. We were just an interlude for those four walls, which had probably seen it all in that time.

I can picture the floorplan of that house perfectly in my head – the hallway, the rooms. The way the walls looked. The front of the house, and the fence between us and our neighbours, the Greens. They were an older white couple, and they were kind to us. They had kids a similar age to Eden and me; we used to play together. And they had a trampoline in the backyard, which was epic for us.

Us kids had a lot of fun in that Neerabup house – on hot days, we'd wash our one of the wheelie bins and fill it with water so it became a (very small!) pool to help us cool down. Eden once broke a finger jumping off the roof of the house – people always described him as a 'tornado' kid, an energetic little tacker, so I have no doubt it was part of a big adventure that went wrong. We didn't always have a lot of supervision at Neerabup, and there would be days sometimes when we wouldn't see Mum if she was using. I remember we had a TV, and staying up late on a mattress on the floor, watching *Rage* all the way into the night.

In this particular memory, I was sitting on the metal frame of a bed in one of the bedrooms. There was no mattress on it, and Mum was perched behind me, a needle in her hand. My arm was up, and she was digging into the skin under my armpit on one side with the needle. I had a lump under there, and she dug away while I winced until – pop! – she flicked a kangaroo tick free. The ticks are a real bugger in parts of Western Australia, and burrow under your skin to suck blood. I remember the tick landing on the bed frame, and then – whack! – Mum slamming it with a shoe, my blood bursting out from its body. I still have the scar on my side.

We'd get boils too, which in our case was from being malnourished. I'd get them on my bum, and Nan or Mum would squeeze them – it hurt so much! I wouldn't be able to sit down properly for ages, and I still have the scars from those as well. My body is like a map of all of these different struggles.

I remember one day, Mum asking me to go next door to the Greens and ask to borrow a spoon, so off I went and got it. I don't know what I thought Mum needed the spoon for at the time, but I'll never forget when I saw it next, lying next to her with her gear, black from the heroin she'd injected. I'm sure the Greens didn't have any idea that's what their spoon would be getting up to either.

Another time, Eden and I climbed over the fence when the Greens were out. We made a beeline for the trampoline – we couldn't resist having it all to ourselves, the freedom to bounce and bounce and bounce without the other kids.

We were both cheeky kids, each other's partner in crime, and somehow, we got into their house. We were only little, both under the age of eight, and I'm sure on some level we knew what we were doing was wrong, but we'd also been to the Greens' house enough times that it probably felt like a grey area, not entirely wrong.

Inside, their house was everything that ours wasn't, in so many ways. Perhaps the biggest difference was just how much *more* they had than us. They weren't rich people – everyone on our street was working class at best, just making ends meet. But they had what I now recognise as a life free from poverty and trauma. At our house, we only had the minimum requirements needed to survive. Meals were often cheap and made in bulk. A treat would be Weetbix with margarine on it, or with jam, if we were lucky enough to have some. Porridge, rice, two-minute noodles: we ate the things that were cheap and filled us up, even if its nutritional value was low. We called it 'povvo' food.

For my entire childhood, my one constant companion was hunger. That sore belly-achey emptiness that gnaws away inside you was a feeling that haunted us all the time. I remember Eden once eating a bit of a meat pie out of a bin on the street, he was so hungry. So it's no surprise that the first thing he and I did when we got inside the Greens' house – walking straight past the Nintendo set, the TV, and the stereo, which an ordinary burglar might have paused at – was head straight to the fridge.

Opening it up was like a scene from a dream. It was *full* of food – milk, cheese, eggs, yoghurt, shiny luscious vegetables, and more. I remember the rush of excitement at the sight of it all, a stark contrast to the grimy, empty shelves that we were used to, with only a few straggling bits and pieces that were slowly going off.

We ate with the fridge door open, hands grabbing things to sample. The pantry was full, too – stacked with cereals we didn't get to eat, packets of biscuits, cans of baked beans. I couldn't believe that right next door there was this absolute treasure, and yet at our place we could spend an entire day having only eaten a single meal, wondering whether it would be another hungry night.

As we were walking through the house on our way out, my eye caught a glimpse of blue in one of the bedrooms. There, on top of the dressing table, was a little palette of blue eye shadow. It was one of those round plastic ones that was common in the '90s – cheap, but probably a luxury to Mrs Green. I loved pretty things like make-up and jewellery – flashy things like nail polish or glitter eye shadow signalled glamour and sophistication to me – and there was nothing like that at our place.

I didn't hesitate long enough to question my decision. I took the eye shadow, and squirrelled it away in my pocket.

In the days that followed, I imagine the Greens knew we'd been in their house. They would have noticed the food that had disappeared from their fridge, the groceries that were moved around in their pantry. Being small children we weren't very good burglars, and I doubt we made an effort to cover our tracks! But they never once brought it up, and they never once begrudged us coming over to use their trampoline or to play with their dog. Maybe that's why they stick so strongly in my memory – the kindness of some stands out against the blurring memories of racism we got from others.

In fact, a lot of my core memories of childhood are hitched to the few people who treated us differently, who showed us respect and compassion. Because, unfortunately, the vast majority of people we dealt with, whether they were social workers, child protection officers, teachers, shop attendants, doctors, even complete strangers, blamed us for our poverty. Or, if they weren't actually hostile, they were indifferent. I can't count the number of times when people turned a blind eye to something they saw happening to us, something that was wrong.

From the moment I could consciously think, I knew that people looked down on my family for being poor. That when a stranger flicked their eyes up and down our bodies, they were taking in our worn-through clothes, and skinny bodies, and dismissing us on that basis. In the eyes of society, being Aboriginal was even worse than just being poor. For a long time, a lot of Australians have believed the story that Indigenous Australians drink, steal, lie and cheat, because that's what they heard about us. That we made bad choices, and that's why we were more likely to be poor, addicts, uneducated, unemployed.

The reality is, when you're living with trauma, from your country being stolen and your culture being stamped out, and when your whole way of life has been destroyed over generations, that changes you. It changes those who come after you, too. Of course, there were many Indigenous people in our community, even members of my own extended family, and close friends, who lived much more middle-class lives. But that's the thing about trauma – it's different for everyone.

When someone in a position of authority showed us kindness, it left a lasting impression on me. I remember watching Mum talking to a child protection worker once, and thinking to myself that something was different about this man.

We regularly dealt with child protection and family services, but this officer spoke to Mum differently, without the frustrated impatience that so many of his colleagues did. He listened to her, and he asked her questions, and addressed her with respect. And it completely flipped my impression of how these moments for my family should play out. It was the first time that I realised that even though my mum was an addict, it didn't mean she didn't deserve the same respect as any other person. That in fact, we all have a right to respect and decency.

I can picture that man clearly. He wore sandals with socks (which even as a child I recognised as a poor fashion choice!), and he was kind. I knew to value that, and I have kept it close for my entire life. Kindness doesn't cost you anything, but God knows, it means a lot to the person who receives it. It's heartbreaking to imagine how differently we would have felt if more of the people who dealt with us had been kind like that man. A cup of tea, a warm smile, even just listening to Mum tell her story, not treating us like criminals or as if we didn't have any choices. Little things made such a big difference when we were going through something that was objectively pretty shit.

The thing that man saw, that many others haven't throughout my life, is that my family were more than our circumstances. As people, as mob, we aren't defined by the things that have held us back, but how we have overcome them. But people rarely see the strength in those who have suffered in their lives.

Yes, my mother had some choice in her addiction. But when the choice is between managing poor mental health with no support, or making yourself feel better in the ways you know how, how do you gather the strength and capacity to make the 'right' choice? Addiction makes it almost impossible to find a job or care for your children. And each of us kids has had to deal with the fall-out of Mum's addiction in our own lives, working through this inheritance as individuals, and that work never ends.

But this is just one side of our multi-sided story. One thing I always knew powerfully was that Mum wanted her children with her, and that she fought for us. Every time we were taken away, she fought fiercely to get us back. Her cycles of addiction came and went, but her love for us was constant.

That's the thing about my life – love, big love, has always been there. The memories of my childhood have as many moments of lightness as they do shade. I remember rolling up with my cousins to the milk bar in Carnarvon to spend our five and ten cent coins on lollies, just like so many other Aussie kids did across the country.

I remember games played with other kids at school, giddy with adrenaline – chasey, kick-to-kick and football games played through backyards and on the street, igniting my love of sport that has been such a big part of who I am for my whole life.

I remember laughing so hard with my brothers that I felt like I couldn't breathe. I remember sleeping tucked up next to Nan, feeling like I was in the safest place in the entire world.

I remember the trips on weekends and in the holidays to the blowholes at Quobba, and Gnaraloo Station – squashed into Mum's old silver Commodore, and running across the pristine white sand of the beach to jump into the turquoise water teeming with fish. Hours of snorkelling and swimming, until the skin on our fingertips were like shrivelled sultanas, and our cheeks hurt from grinning. As water people, the blowholes were such an important place for us, and those trips were special on so many levels. The feeling of being grounded on country was one of the best things ever.

It's these moments that I hold close in my heart, that make me ache with homesickness when I'm away, and which remind me who I am when I find myself questioning it. I am the sum of so many parts, but family, country, and culture are the foundations that can never be shaken.

Two

The only thing that was a constant in my childhood was that I was always moving. I moved between my mum and my nan and my dad, between Carnarvon, Quairading and Perth, from house to house, from bed to bed, from school to school. Each place was completely different, a new reality to wake up to, and I became pretty adept at switching, where at one there'd be a house full of passing strangers, no food, and the cops showing up when a fight broke out, and at the next I'd get three meals a day and a bath before bed.

But staying with Nan always felt like a break from those stark shifts. When I was about eight, Mum moved us from Neerabup in Perth, to Carnarvon, nine hours north, where she grew up, and Nan came with us too. But from time to time, Nan would go back to Quairading to see her sisters and to be on country, and often I would go and stay with her there, with one or another of my siblings.

When I went to stay with Nan in Quairading, I always felt really special. She taught me foundation skills I wasn't getting from Mum or Dad. I always say that Nan taught me how to make a bed, how to cook, how to clean, and how to paint. And she could really paint, Nan – beautiful animals like dolphins and sea turtles. I'd sit with her, learning from watching her. Her house in Quairading was a cute little cottage, probably government housing, although I wasn't old enough at the time to know. Nan would put the woodfire stove on, and the smoky scent made the house smell really cozy. Then she'd make damper, put the kettle on, and settle down to paint.

Nan used paddle pop sticks to paint with – she'd dip the end in paint and let it dry, and do that again and again until there was a kind of blobby tip to the stick, and then she'd use that to do her dot painting. She'd get deep in her concentration when she was painting, and I'd sit next to her on the couch, watching. The couch at Nan's was so uncomfortable – it was leather, which I hated, because it got so cold (and I still hate leather couches to this day) – but I was mesmerised, and I'd sit quietly and still to watch her work. I especially liked how meticulous she was about the textures she created. She'd place the dot and then lift the stick so that a little peak of paint would form, and she made sure all the peaks were a uniform shape across the painting. If one wasn't right, she'd go back, a little frown on her face, and correct it until it matched.

I paint and make art myself now, in fact the image behind me on the cover of this book is my own, inspired by my family and mob and the colours I love. Painting makes me feel closer to Nan, and reminds me of the yarns she'd tell me when she working. I think making art made her feel more connected to culture and country. It was Nan who told me the story of the turtles coming to swim around Mum when she was swimming at the Bluff at Quobba Station when I was in the womb. Nan was on the shore, watching Mum swim, and saw the turtles popping up around her. Nan was the one who gave me the sea turtle, the Buyungurra, as my totem.

Everything I learned about culture and country come from my nan, and a lot of that is still with me now. Her special stew and her chicken noodle soup recipes are also still with me – I always make those dishes when I feel homesick, and when the grief for Nan is especially strong.

Nan's house was a happy place for me and my brothers when we stayed with her. She made us tea (dinner), we were clean and cared for, and we had comfortable beds to sleep in. I didn't mind staying with my dad, but I missed my family when I was away from them for too long. Dad lived in Armadale, a suburb in the south-west of Perth, with his partner Leanne – they had been together from as early as I can remember, and I have brothers on that side of the family, Tye and Kallom.

I was always taken care of when I stayed at Dad's, but his feelings about Mum weren't positive. As a kid you sense that kind of tension, and I never felt fully relaxed at his place. Even though living with Mum was chaotic and there was never any guarantee I'd get fed, make it to school, or that Mum wouldn't be on a bender, or be out of it – or even in one of her angry moods – I still wanted to be there, with her and the rest of my family.

While we were living with Mum, sometimes we went in and out of foster care. There was always the possibility that we would be taken away, and Mum feared it constantly. Like most addicts, Mum was always up and down. When she was on a sober streak, she'd really try and get her shit together, and for a little while, we'd have better food, and she'd tidy the house, and we'd visit the blowholes and swim in the ocean together.

We'd feel like a real family, then, all of us together. But as soon as she started using again, things would quickly get messy. One night she'd be out partying, and the next she'd be in her room with the door shut, often for days. Sometimes she just didn't come home. Other times, the drugs would make her mean, violent even.

The threat of us being split up and taken away reared its head most during these times, when Mum was too far gone to deal with it. I remember this happening at the Neerabup house, the one next door to the Greens. Sometimes Mum wasn't around for days at a time, and it was just me and my brothers at home. Ky was out of school by this point, just a young teen herself, and I reckon she was already using drugs too. Troy was just a baby then, and I was only about five.

When Mum was at home, she'd often have friends over, and sometimes things would get out of control, everyone getting rowdy while they were all high or out of it. The cops would turn up a fair bit. Our house was even on the news one night, after police were called there because of a violent incident. I was too young to remember what happened, but the Neerabup place was like a halfway house – people came and went, and there were always adults hanging around who we didn't know very well.

Back then, Eden and I spent a lot of time together, finding ways to stay out of trouble, or to start trouble, depending on our mood. On this particular day, he jumped off the roof of the house, and this is when he broke his finger, his pinky. I swear, it's a miracle that boy survived childhood. He was always getting up to something, but for a little guy he was also tough. Again, because I was so young, I don't recall what he was doing on the roof, but that was the kind of thing we did a lot, testing the boundaries when there was so little supervision.

Tough or not, the way Eden was screaming when he came off the roof, I knew it was serious. And when Mum heard the noise and came out, she freaked. Eden was crying, and Mum was saying we couldn't go to the hospital – that if we did, officials would start asking questions, and take us kids away. So we didn't go to the hospital, and we never, ever called the police or for an ambulance when things went wrong.

You can probably gather from now that a lot of the timeline of my early childhood is blurry – because moving was a constant, it's shuffled the chronology in my head, though there's a clear marker from when I was about eight, when we moved north to Carnarvon more permanently. Before then, though, we lived in a few places around Perth and there's one memory that stands out in particular, because that's when Troy's dad died.

His name was also Troy – Troy Senior – and he and Mum had a pretty fiery relationship. When they were sober, life seemed to be on an even keel, but when Mum was using, she could be quite violent. We'd get flogged, and her partner would get flogged, too – which sounds strange, but Seanna was a force to be reckoned with. Like Mum, Troy Senior was an addict, so he and Mum were both often out of it, and they didn't always remember what went on when they were high.

One night, I wet the bed. I remember waking up, and the sheets being wet. I was only about five, so I did what any other kid that age would do – I got out of bed and went looking for an adult. Sometimes Mum wouldn't be home at night, but this time she was. I walked into her room, where she and Troy were sleeping, passed out on a mattress.

I don't know how I knew it, but I could tell Troy Senior was dead. I found out later that he had overdosed. It was the first time I saw a dead body.

When I think about these moments from my childhood, I can see why we were taken away by child protection. Not that many five-year-olds discover dead adults when they're just looking for someone to comfort them in the middle of the night. But that's what our lives were like – one minute we were kids, the next minute we were seeing and doing things that most adults don't have to deal with.

When we moved to Carnarvon, Eden stayed in Perth with Grandma Susette to start high school, and there were a few years when I don't remember seeing him. He'd later move up north to Onslow to live on country with his dad and his mob there. Grandma Susette deserves a special mention, because she was one of the many people who weren't technically related to us, but who became as important to us as family. Grandma Susette was white, which makes it even more unusual that she would take in an Aboriginal child who wasn't her own.

We knew Susette because one of her sons was good friends with Troy Senior. Mum met Susette through Troy, and they became close friends. She was a very kind woman, full of care and energy, despite the fact she'd lost one of her legs from the knee down to cancer, and we'd often stay with her when we were visiting in Perth. It's funny to think how, even though there was so much movement and inconsistency in our lives, the thing that always held strong were relationships we had with people like Grandma Susette, who to us was like a guardian angel or Mother Theresa.

In Carnarvon, we were surrounded by family, so that meant that even when Mum was high or out of the house for days at a time, there were still people around to keep an eye on us. Ky was in her own world, so I spent a lot of time with Troy and taking care of RJ, my youngest brother who was born by then. RJ's dad, Dragan, was of Eastern European heritage, though I'm not sure of his actual ethnicity. He was a nice guy when he was around, and he lived with us most of the time in Carnarvon.

It was around this time that I realised that child protection could come and take us away at any moment.

'See them cars with the blue licence plates?' Mum told us, pointing at a government car parked down the road when we were driving back from town one day. 'You see one of them, you go hide, OK? They'll come to take you kids away, so you gotta hide in the storeroom where they won't find you.'

The storeroom was a cupboard in the hallway, and we could just about squeeze in there, the three of us. We'd crouch there all squashed together, waiting for whoever was at the front door to give up, or for the adults to stop talking. And sometimes we'd play games in there.

I loved school, and my brothers tell me that I used to make them into my students in the storeroom, and write on the back of the cupboard door with Texta so we could practise the alphabet and numbers. I was bossy, even as a little one, and clearly I never wasted an opportunity to be in charge of my brothers!

Mum was gone a lot during this time, and if anyone ever asked me where she was, I used to say 'Driving,' because she was often out cruising the streets in her old silver Commodore. I remember the rush of excitement I felt whenever I saw it roll up. Sometimes she'd pull up beside me and Troy and our cousins (Aunty Katrina's and Aunty Ricki's kids) when we were walking home from school.

'Get in!' she'd shout with a grin, and we'd cheer, clambering inside and fighting over who got to ride shotgun.

Sometimes she'd take us past the milk bar and we'd get lollies. Every so often, she'd catch us in the morning before school and pull a few coins out from somewhere like magic so we could buy lunch at the canteen. Those days were the best – we were so used to going hungry.

On the days where there was no lunch money, I used to hang around the teachers' lounge at school and hope that they had something for me to eat. Other times, Troy and I would go to the breakfast club at school and we'd scarf as much as we could, never missing the chance for a free feed. We didn't always have the right school uniform, either, so the ladies at the front office would rummage around in the lost-and-found basket and quickly pull something together for us both from whatever had been left there over the last week.

My early education was pretty patchy, because if I was staying with Dad in Perth, he'd enrol me at a school nearby. I reckon I went to dozens of primary schools all up, sometimes for just a few days, or a few weeks at a time at the most. When we were living in Neerabup, and our grandad on Mum's side was spending a little more time with us, I even went to a Muslim school briefly, which must have been partly because of his Malaysian heritage. Dad saw me come home wearing the uniform and a hijab, and he was not happy. He ripped the hijab off me right away, and that was the end of Muslim school.

I missed a lot of school, too – because we were moving, or I had to stay home and take care of the boys, or it was just that there wasn't anyone to tell me to go. As a very young child, I didn't always know how to get myself up and off to school without supervision. It's no wonder Ky dropped out of school when she did, because no one was keeping an eye on our attendance.

In Carnarvon, we knew most of the other kids who went to school with us, and I'd hang out at different houses in the afternoons. There was a lot of poverty in Carnarvon, but there were also a lot of people living much more 'normal' lives than us. Even other mob, like my friend Skyla and her family, had middle-class lives that were nothing like mine. Whenever I visited I was always gobsmacked by all the stuff they had, and how ordered and neat their house was.

I had another friend whose parents were a lesbian couple, a rarity in Carnarvon, who certainly weren't out (everyone thought they were just best friends). They had a real soft spot for me, and I would hang out at their place after school and then leave reluctantly at dinner time. They were always coming up with reasons for me to stay longer, no doubt to get a meal into me if that was the least they could do. But I knew I was just a visitor in their world, so I'd trudge back home to see if there was a meal for dinner, or if there was anything in the kitchen and fridge to cobble together.

People knew we were poor, but they really didn't get it. When we didn't have anything to eat at school, friends would sometimes ask, 'Why can't your mum just give you lunch money?' I never knew what to say back. Adults understood better, and they knew that we were on our own a lot at home, but at the same time, no one really did anything about it.

Troy and I became our own little unit then. We were each other's best friends, and worst enemies, depending on the day. I'll always remember one fight we had in particular, because it landed us younger kids in foster care for a long time.

I don't know how it started, but it ended with Troy stabbing me in the ankle with a butter knife. A butter knife! I still have the scar, so he must have come at me pretty hard for it to cut me like it did. At the time, we were staying on a plantation – Mum and Dragan would work on farms picking vegetables and fruit around Carnarvon, and sometimes we'd stay in the accommodation they had on site. Mum would even get us to help pick the veggies, and we'd get $5 for a day of picking (which in retrospect was a rip off, but at the time it felt like a fortune).

At one of the farms, we would stay in a cabin, which had a bedroom, a bathroom, and a kitchenette, and it also had a computer. Troy and I argued all the time about whose turn it was to use the computer, because we both wanted to play Minesweeper on it. (Other '90s kids will appreciate that reference – it was the first computer game most of us got into.)

Most of our arguments ended up with us chasing each other around, screaming and yelling. Now, one of the best things about staying on the plantations was how much fresh food there was to eat – the seconds that were left over after the quality produce got packed onto the trucks. It also meant a fair few food fights for us kids. Once Troy threw a rotten capsicum at me, and I ducked, thinking it would go over my head, but instead I copped it straight to my face. Capsicum sludge was everywhere, and I still struggle to eat capsicum now without feeling like I'm going to retch.

This time though, Troy went for a butter knife from the kitchenette, and I ran into the bathroom to try and hide from him. There were already holes in the wall; it was a pretty run-down place. In the end he got in and we tussled, and I ended up stabbed in the ankle.

I cried bloody murder, and Mum came storming out of her room. She grabbed the broom and really gave it to Troy, flogging him with the stick. There was yelling and shouting, and Troy was screaming, and soon it became clear that Mum had hit Troy so hard that she'd broken his arm.

Mum was furious, and she didn't want to take Troy to the hospital, for the same reason she wouldn't take Eden when he broke his finger. The last thing we needed was for the do-gooder social workers to get into our business. Mum might have flogged us, but she was still our mother, and family was better than strangers, no matter what. To us, being flogged didn't seem so out of the ordinary anyway, because everyone else around us copped it, including us. Adults flogged each other, kids flogged kids – violence was just an everyday part of life, so we didn't really understand why child protection would take us away from Mum for that reason.

The longer we left it, though, the worse Troy's arm got, and eventually he could barely move it. Mum had to take him to the hospital then, and that time she somehow managed to avoid any curly questions by officials. Like most kids his age, Troy's tears dried up pretty quickly once he had a cast on, which he thought made him look pretty cool.

When we went back to school soon after, he was flaunting it all over the place in the playground.

'*Shut up*,' I kept hissing at him. 'Don't make a big deal out of it!' No one had told me to lie about how my brother broke his arm, but instinct was telling me that this was one of those things that other people didn't need to know about.

'Oi, what happened to your arm, Troy?' one of the kids called out.

'He fell off his bike,' I said, but Troy was way ahead of me.

'Nah, I didn't,' he shouted back. 'My mum flogged me!'

Well, that was the end of that. One of the teachers heard, and they had mandatory reporting obligations, so it wasn't long before Troy and I were taken out of class to the front office, where we were to await our fate. My heart was already sinking; I knew it wasn't going to be good. I think Troy started to get it once the child protection officers came, because it became very clear very quickly that we weren't going home.

We were put in the back of a car and taken to the foster home that was waiting for us. Little RJ was picked up and brought to the foster house separately, and it still hurts to try and picture that devastating scene, Mum's baby being taken from her. She would have been distraught.

We didn't see Mum for a while after that.

Our foster carers, Ken and Barb, were an older couple, grandparent age. They weren't our first – we were taken away at least once before, when Troy Senior died, but because I was so young I don't remember much. But I do remember the feeling I had then, of dread and homesickness, and fear.

But Ken and Barb were lovely and kind, and from the moment we walked into their house I knew that our life would be different there. Their house was what we thought was posh, and I even had my own room, a luxury I hadn't had before, space all to myself. It was a little like being with Nan when we stayed with her in Quairading; an in-between place where it was clean, warm, with good food and routine. But unlike Nan's, it wasn't home. Ken and Barb were good people, but they weren't family, and Troy and I knew that it wasn't permanent.

Every morning, I'd make my bed and tidy my room. I took so much pride in it – and that sense of house pride has stayed with me, because even now my home is always calm and spotless and neat, everything with a place and a purpose. I guess being raised in chaos left its mark on me. Even though Ken and Barb treated me like a child, I still felt I had to take care of my brothers, and I'd try and keep their rooms neat too, and remind them of their manners.

We did activities that I hadn't done before, things other kids probably took for granted as part of an ordinary childhood. One day Barb and I made a mulberry pie together in the kitchen. I'd never baked anything before, but at home I cooked all the time, like porridge on the stove, if that's what you could call cooking. There were a few mulberry trees on Ken and Barb's property, and I'd told Barb about how we'd often pick mulberries from the trees on our way to school, a free feed – us kids would strip the fruit from the trees and eat handfuls of them every year when they were in season. Our fingers would get all stained from the juice, and we knew that if you needed to get the stains out you could get a green, unripe mulberry and rub it over your skin to clean it. While I was something of a mulberry connoisseur, I'd never cooked with them before, let alone baked a pie.

I went and picked the berries, and then Barb set up the kitchen and showed me how to knead the dough, how to roll it out, how to pinch the edges of the pie with my fingertips to make it pretty. It sounds like such a wholesome memory now, but I felt so restless. It didn't feel right to be doing something like this – even though it was fun, I was still homesick, and I missed Mum. After a while, Mum was able to visit, but only with Ken and Barb there, and it just wasn't the same as having her all to ourselves. At night, even though I was cozy in my bed, and safe in my own room, I still felt a deep bellyache of sadness. It was so confusing, and it must have been even harder for the boys, being as young as they were. I still can't imagine what RJ would have felt as a toddler, his whole world changing so dramatically.

But the most bizarre thing about being fostered by Ken and Barb was that they lived practically across the road from our place. Mum and Nan had no idea that's where we were, but if I went to the end of Ken and Barb's property, I could see our house.

Their property was a decent size; they used quad bikes to get around on it, and at the far end there were mangrove trees, and a ditch, and then the road. One day, Troy and I were playing high up in the trees, and I caught sight of a familiar figure in the backyard across the road, hanging up laundry. It was Nan. I couldn't believe it – she was right there, only 50 metres away – I could have dashed that distance in no time and hugged her. I could have shouted her name, and she would have come running.

For some reason, though, I couldn't bring myself to call out. My voice died in my throat. Maybe I knew it would cause trouble; that they weren't allowed to come and get us. Maybe I just felt funny about being trapped between two different lives, where I could see the good things about living with Ken and Barb, but I wanted home more than anything else in the world. I still don't know why I didn't call out – why do kids do what they do? But I can still picture that moment in my mind: Nan at the clothesline, not knowing that her grandkids were just within reach.

Eventually we did go home, and it was bittersweet. Mum would always fight to have us back, and when she was going through a good patch she'd really turn things around. She knew she had to prove to the authorities that she could take care of her kids – and that she loved us and she wanted us – but it was only a matter of time before she started using again, and life went back to the usual chaos.

The hardest thing was that when it was bad, sometimes it was really, *really* bad. There was one time in particular when Mum's violence meant she almost lost custody of me for good.

When Mum was coming down, she'd stay in her room for days and days. It would be dark in there, the curtains always closed, the air stale and musty, and she'd leave the TV on while she slept.

One day, I was running late for school. I would have been between eight or nine years old, and I went into Mum's room to ask for lunch money to spend at the canteen. Mum would usually find a few coins if she had them. If she had nothing, we got nothing, but I'd always ask. Sometimes we'd get a real treat if she had some goldies left over from the night before, and if she came up empty, I'd be hustling for the leftovers of my friends' lunches, or hanging around the teachers' lounge again.

In her room, Mum was just a shape lying under the bedcovers. She was so small – I barely ever saw her eat anything herself – but her mass of thick black hair told me she was there, maybe asleep, maybe just ignoring me.

I was whingeing. She hated it when I whinged, and I was probably extra annoying because I hadn't seen her for a few days.

'Mum, you got any money?'

'Muum, I need lunch money, I'm late for school.'

'*Muuuuuum.*'

When I didn't get a reaction, I crept all the way up to her, and touched her on the shoulder, hoping to wake her up. Now, if there was one thing I usually knew *not* to do, it was to get up in Mum's space when she was coming down. But I forgot, and I paid the price for it.

She snarled, and in a flash, she flung out her leg and kicked me. I went flying. I was only little, very light, and the force of her kick sent me sprawling through the air. I whacked hard against the TV with my back, and the impact felt as if someone had shot me in the spine.

It hurt so much, I wailed and cried, and I knew the noise would only annoy Mum more, so after a while, I dragged myself up and did my best to get to school. There was no one to run to, no one to ask to make it better. I knew I had to sort it out myself, so off I went, struggling to walk with the pain, and tears streaming down my face.

I don't know how long it took me to walk to school. My back was burning with pain. Looking back, my tailbone was either very badly bruised or even fractured. It was agony to walk, and it was even worse sitting down.

Somehow I shuffled all the way to school, sat painfully through class, and watched the other kids play netball from the sidelines at lunchtime, because there was no way I could do that. I didn't know how to ask for help – and if I told a teacher about what had happened, we'd probably all get taken away again. As for anyone noticing that I was in pain, I was good at slipping under the radar and staying out of trouble. I must have hidden it well, because no one did anything at the time.

A little while later, I went to stay with Dad and Leanne in Perth, and they could tell something was wrong from the way I was walking and sitting.

'What's happened to you?' Dad asked.

I couldn't think of a lie, so I told the truth. 'Mum booted me.'

The next thing, all hell broke loose. Dad was mad, as if he'd been waiting for something like this to happen; he was always asking about Mum when I saw him. He'd forget to ask me things about my own life, like school, sport, even just how I was going, but on every visit, he'd ask about what Mum was up to. I'd shrug and say what I always said: 'She's been driving.'

But the way Dad reacted to my injury, he was like a vindicated man, finally proven right. All of a sudden he was on the phone, lodging a complaint with the child protection services, filling out forms. I had to make a statement, and I found the whole process completely terrifying. I didn't want Mum to get in trouble, but I was also scared and hurt, and seeing how these adults reacted confirmed for me that it wasn't OK for Mum to physically hurt me.

With each new phone call, and with each new official who asked me to give a statement, and with each new examination of my back, I could feel stress and worry building up inside me. Dad wanted to get custody, but that didn't make sense to me either, because to me he hadn't always been the most caring father. I felt sick thinking about how Mum would react.

In the end, it all came to a head when I had to meet with child protection officers for an interview. The woman doing the interview is seared into my memory, because for some reason she really scared me. She was just another person from the government, and in my short life I'd met plenty, but this time I felt anxious, and after a little while I broke down in tears.

'I want Mum,' I cried. 'I want to go back to Mum.'

And that was that. Not too long after, I was back in Carnarvon with Mum.

There was no getting around the violence at home, though. It was intense. We kids had a sense of humour about it, because it happened a lot and we'd learned to cope with it. Troy and I would joke about it, though we knew it wasn't normal. I knew that other families didn't have the kind of fights mine did, and that other mums weren't as volatile as mine, but I didn't fully understand that what we suffered was abuse until I grew up.

Even little things could trigger a violent response. Every child nicks money from their parents at some stage, and once I stole $16 out of Mum's wallet. I don't know what I was thinking, except it wasn't with my brain – it was definitely with my stomach. I bought $16 worth of lollies in town, and I tell you what, I was like a total hustler with the other kids. I don't think I'd ever been more popular!

When I got home, I tried to play it cool, but Mum had figured it out, and she was raging. I grabbed my backpack and bolted out of the house, shouting that I wasn't coming back. I ran across the road, and I could hear her shouting after me, but I knew she wouldn't give chase.

The only problem was, I hadn't thought my plan through, and now I was a little kid out in the dark, and as mob will know, that made me a prime target for a featherfoot, or a wood archie, as we also knew them. Every culture has a devil spirit, and for the Noongar people, the featherfoot is a monster that comes out and snatches kids after dark to eat. We were always told that we had to be home before dark, otherwise the wood archies would get us. They had bright red eyes that would watch us in the dark, and it would send shivers up our spines thinking of them lurking out there waiting to grab us.

Uncle Pinhead knew how freaked out we were by the wood archies, so he'd spin yarns all the time. 'Yeah, I've been in fights with them,' he'd boast. 'Could've died! But I'm strong, I fought them off. Still got the scars and everything!'

We'd be wide-eyed with awe at how strong our uncle was to survive a brawl with a wood archie!

That night, I tried to string out my escape from Mum and find my courage, knowing full well if I went home it would be for a flogging. I could still taste the lollies on my tongue, but weighing up my options, I figured it was a smarter long-term plan to just go and take my punishment, rather than risk being snatched by a monster in the dark.

I did get flogged, but the lollies were totally worth it. I reckon Mum secretly felt a bit of pride in my ability to take the flogging too, even when I knew it was coming. That kind of violence, when it happened, wasn't really scary for me. It was just how it was in our house – actions had consequences, and sometimes those consequences were extreme.

But the kick, and the way my tailbone hurt, that *did* scare me. Mum didn't really seem to care when she kicked me, and I'd never suffered pain like that before. But then I was home again, and we just moved on from it.

I'll never know if Mum knew that Dad had wanted custody of me, or what life could have been like if I'd agreed to stay with Dad and Leanne. But I also didn't know then that I'd only have Mum with me for a few more years.

Maybe there was a part of me, some older knowledge inside of me, that knew that our time was limited. Mum wasn't an easy woman to live with, and she wasn't the most caring mother, but she was my mum. And truth be told, I loved her, and she loved us.

I couldn't leave her then, and knowing now what was coming, I'm so grateful that I didn't.

Three

If my memories of being a kid are mixed up, I think I can pinpoint exactly when they sharpen further into full focus. I was around eleven years old, and that year was a huge turning point in my life. It was the year that Mum died.

For some people, a turning point is a happy thing, when things suddenly change for the better. You hear those stories of the singer or actor who gets 'discovered' – they become famous and everything about their lives gets bigger, better, flashier. But for me, most of the big turning points in my life have been surrounded by urgency and where the choices are between everything falling apart, or someone or something intervening and changing the path in front of me.

That's the thing about poverty – there's a very small gap between just scraping by, and falling down into a black hole of hopelessness, and I have been mighty lucky in my life that every time I was about to fall – when I was teetering on the very edge – someone reached out and pulled me back.

Here's what I remember about the time before Seanna left us.

For a decent stretch of time, long enough that it made an impression on me even back then, Mum was in a good place.

When she was pregnant with RJ, she stayed off the drugs. It's as if she could never resist them when it was just herself she was hurting, but the baby made her stay strong. She wasn't perfect – she was still smoking cigarettes, and I don't know if she stopped drinking. But without the drugs, life at home was less chaotic. She was around more, and she and Dragan were good together.

Pretty soon after Mum gave birth to RJ, though, the bad habits crept back in. It wasn't long before she was using again, coming and going from the house, and mean and violent when she was coming down. I remember once she took to someone with a baseball bat, chasing them around, screaming and bashing, while they yelped every time they got hit: 'Oi-oi-oi!' To us it sounded funny; that kind of violence was normal for us. We couldn't see how wrong it was, because Mum was just like that. She'd bash someone on the street if they picked a fight with her. When she dropped me at Dad's place, I'd seen her abuse Leanne, even smash the windows of her car once; and of course she'd even hurt us.

It's really hard to reconcile how much I loved Mum – and how much I knew without a doubt in the world that she loved us – with how violent she could be. When she was on drugs, it was just a rollercoaster of Seanna, and there was nothing else to do but go with it. I guess we learned to get out of her way early on, so we wouldn't get caught in it.

When Mum was about eight months pregnant with RJ, my sister Kyandra found out she was pregnant too. Ky was sixteen, and hardly ever home. She always with her boyfriend, Shane, the older brother of my friend Skyla, and staying at his house. His folks weren't thrilled that Ky was pregnant. She was already on drugs, following in Mum's footsteps. It's hard to think back to

Ky then, taking the first steps on a journey that was going to lead to a very hard life for her. I often wonder what could have been on the cards for Ky if she'd had a different start, or more options given to her, because I always knew my big sister was special.

I completely idolised Ky. When we were living in the Neerabup house, I was only little, and Ky would get me ready for school. She'd brush my hair out, sitting behind me on the bed, and help me get dressed, showing me the same tenderness that I went on to show my younger brothers.

Ky was cheeky as a teenager, and a carbon copy of Mum in her looks. If you remember the '90s television sitcom *My Wife and Kids*, people would always say that Ky looked like the character Claire Kyle, played by the actor Jazz Raycole. Ky had long curly hair, a beautiful face, and she was good at everything she put her hand to. She was a great dancer, and for a while at school, she played golf, and had even competed in a tournament once. I have no idea how this happened or how she accessed the gear for it, but I was so proud of my big sister, the golf star!

But at some point, Ky hit a turning point herself that set her on a distinctly destructive path. She started dabbling in drugs really young, probably around twelve or thirteen years old. In a way, Ky and Eden copped the worst of Mum's addiction because they were the eldest of the kids in our family. There wasn't a lot of guidance for them – no one telling Ky to stay off the drugs, or checking that she was going to school. So it wasn't long before Ky fell out of the school system, and then she fell pregnant. It was as if she was repeating the same path that Mum took. Mum was sixteen when she had Ky.

But just like Mum, while Ky was pregnant, she quit the drugs. She took care of her body, because it was holding life, and we all knew that life is sacred. But again, much like Mum, once the baby was born, she couldn't resist the pull of her addiction, and the cycle started again.

We were visiting family on the outskirts of Perth when Ky went into labour. We rushed her to a small regional hospital in Northam, and I was there, along with Mum and Aunty Brenda. I remember the astringent smell of the hospital, and being absolutely shocked and overwhelmed by what was happening in front of me. Ky was up on the bed, and Mum and Aunty Brenda were supporting her, and I watched as my nephew's head was squeezed from my sister like a miracle. It was both beautiful and completely horrifying to my eleven-year-old self.

'See, girl, this is what happens if you have sex!' Aunty Brenda said, never one to miss a chance to scare some sense into one of her nieces or daughters.

I thought I was going to faint and had to leave the room, but the sights and sounds of the delivery were enough for me, and I vowed then and there that if that was what came after sex, I was happy to stay a virgin forever!

Ky and Mum decided to call the baby Wraith, after a ghost character in a scary movie that Mum loved. So he was named Wraith Shane Blurton, but eventually that got changed officially to just Shane, after his dad, and we called him Bubba Shane. So, along with RJ, there were two babies in our family, almost a year apart, and two mothers who weren't able to give them what they needed.

With Mum back in her destructive cycle, she wasn't capable of looking after RJ, so from the moment he was born, I took care of my baby brother. I was nine when RJ was born, and with Mum coming and going as she was, and Nan, who was now too unwell to care for him, I knew I had to step in. I was a skinny little thing, but I was smart, and I'd watched Mum enough to remember and mimic her actions. I boiled bottles on the stove to sterilise them, and I knew to scoop the powdered formula into them, add water and shake the bottle until the powder mingled and dissolved, to make the milk that my little brother sucked up so greedily. I would microwave the bottle, and squirt a little on my wrist, like I'd seen Mum do, testing the temperature. I was so young, but I was strong enough to hold my brother, and feed him on my lap.

I changed RJ's nappies, and put him to bed, and even bathed him. I remember trying to fill the tub to give him a bath once, then discovered that our gas bottle had run out and there wasn't money to get another. So I boiled water in the kettle, and mixed it with cold water in the laundry trough. I wasn't tall enough to reach him properly from outside the tub so I climbed in there with my shorts and T-shirt still on so I could bathe him, scooping water with my fingers, and wiping down his little brown baby's body.

But I couldn't care for Bubba Shane too. I don't have a lot of memories of him, and he was removed from Ky's care when he was quite young. Ky was using drugs again so she was often out of it, and she was quite rough with her little baby. It wasn't long before Shane Senior, his father, got full custody, and they lived down the road from us, so we still saw Bubba Shane occasionally.

I remember Ky clearly at that time, because there was a strange kind of 'mirroring' behaviour going on between her and Mum. If one of them started sinking, the other one did too, them each spiralling with their addiction and poor mental health. Years later, Ky was diagnosed with schizophrenia, which made a lot of sense of her earlier life, once we knew. And truth be told, Ky was visibly sinking into a hole. She was spaced out and disconnected. I remember her wearing a particular pair of grey tracksuit pants that were too big for her skinny hips, and they'd slide down all the time. She wasn't showering, or taking care of herself. She wasn't in any state to take care of her baby, or to look out for any of us, either.

So life at home was really dark in a lot of ways. I was spending a lot of time with Nan, who was living with us in Carnarvon all the time then, and her health was deteriorating. She'd become very frail very quickly, and her mobility wasn't great. I became like a full-time carer, washing her, massaging the liniment into her tired old joints, making sure she was eating, and using my body like a crutch to help her move around the house, between her bed and the garden. She was a big woman − over six feet tall and over 100 kilos in weight, so it wasn't easy for me as a kid to be caring for her, but I loved doing it. It made me feel close to her.

I'd also count out her pills for her in the morning − by then, she was on so many different kinds of medication − for diabetes, blood pressure; you name it, she was on it. I'd bring the tablets to her with a cup of tea, where she was sitting outside in the garden in 'her' chair, one of those ubiquitous dark green plastic moulded seats, or in front of the telly. She didn't have the kind of energy she did when we were younger. Back then, the yarns would just pour out of her, but she wasn't as talkative anymore. It was as if life had finally caught up with her.

Nan had a hard life. She knew a thing or two about proper hard yakka, real work, and having to make a life for herself, even when everything was stacked against her. I don't know as much as I wish I did about Nan's life, but the bits and pieces I do tell me that she was never given the chance to live her truth, or reach her potential, because she was Aboriginal, and a woman – two things that meant the people with all the power couldn't see any value in her.

She was denied an education, and for a long time she worked as a domestic servant for a white family. She was a proud woman, and she always kept her house as beautifully as she could. I remember her teaching me how to make a bed properly, with sharp corners and the sheets pulled tight so it all looked neat and crisp.

One of twelve kids, Nan had five herself, and there was heartache there – her oldest son, my Uncle Murray, died before I really knew him. Uncle Ronald (Uncle Pinhead), lived with us for most of the time we were in Carnarvon. As you'll have discovered already, he was a bit of a larrikin, and full of stories. People used to call him Freezeman, too, because there was this yarn that he was once declared dead by the cops after a bender one night, and woke up in the morgue! I don't know how true the story was, but Uncle Pinhead was a bit of a legend around the place.

And there was Uncle Derek and Aunty Coral, and Mum as the youngest. Five children, five fathers who didn't provide. Nan wasn't able to keep everyone together, but she and Mum were inseparable, and I can see the similarities in them more and more now that I'm older and can look back with clearer hindsight. Even though she was always at Mum about her drug use, Nan was an addict herself, an alcoholic, and like Mum, she could get mean when she was under the influence. Never once to me, but when the booze hit her, it was as if the old wounds got opened up, and some of the hurt and pain of her life came pouring out.

Those moments weren't frequent enough to make an impact on me though. I remember Nan as the woman who taught me so much about life, and family, and how to be a good woman and bring people together. Once she taught Troy and me how to make papier-mâché moneyboxes. She showed us how to rip up newspaper and use craft glue to layer it up over a balloon and let it harden and set. Then we cut up egg cartons and used them to make little legs, and she helped us paint our creations into a pig and a penguin, then cut a slit in the top. I got the penguin, which I was excited about, especially painting his white belly.

'See here – you take the money you earn and put it into this money box,' Nan instructed. 'Then, when it's nice and heavy, you can smash it and spend all that money you saved.'

I listened wide-eyed. Truly, that was the first and only lesson in personal finance I ever got when I was growing up!

Nan taught us other things too, especially in the garden, though it wasn't much of one in the traditional sense. I'd been over to my friends' houses and had seen what a beautiful garden could look like, with landscaping and flowers and mulch, everything pretty and ordered. Our garden was just a patch of grass out the front of the house with a tangle of bushes, and out back it was mostly sand, with a little straggly area of grass and some big trees. But Nan tended to those two patches of nature with all her care. She'd get me and Troy out there with her, each of us with a plastic bag, and set us to weeding, though truth be told, we were always thinking, 'What's the point? They'll all be back next week!' But we'd pull those weeds for Nan, because she loved that garden and we'd do anything for her.

Sitting in her favourite chair, she was a pretty formidable sight: a tall, proud blak woman, with the garden hose in one hand, her thumb placed strategically to turn the trickle of water into a spray, and a ciggie in the other. There she'd sit, watering her 'lawn', always dressed neatly with her watch and her special ring on. She was really particular about wearing them, she always wore both. I have them now, and they're so special to me.

Sometimes she'd wander the backyard with us and teach us some of its little secrets, like how to suck the sweet nectar from honeysuckle flowers for a free, sweet treat. Or she'd pull eucalyptus leaves off the trees, crush them up and get us to breathe the scent in deeply from her hands. 'Blackfella Vicks,' she'd say, grinning, and our sinuses would feel fresh and clean.

Thinking on it now, it's weird to realise that Nan was actually only in her sixties then. My adult brain can't reconcile how young she would have been to have five adult kids, and how old she seemed then, struggling to move around her home and needing my care. Understandably, Nan had a very strong mistrust of institutions – she never went to the doctor or the hospital if she could help it. Growing up when she did, with mob being put into missions, being separated from their families, she didn't have a good feeling about government services – she didn't even have the right to vote until she was twenty-seven years old, in 1967. I don't know if she would have had better health with more medical intervention, because trauma has its impact on the body, and she was carrying a lot.

The day that Nanna had her stroke, she was in the back garden, sitting in her chair. I was inside the house, and maybe Uncle Pinhead was there, sleeping off a big night in one of the bedrooms, but I can't remember now. Troy was probably playing somewhere outside in the street, and I can't place where RJ was; perhaps Mum had taken him with her when she'd left for the day, driving off in the Commodore with him strapped into the baby seat we got from who-knows-where.

I went outside into the backyard, checking on Nan as I often did. Sometimes she'd call for me from the garden: 'Brookey, make us a cuppa!' But that morning she was quiet. Maybe that's what made me go and check on her, as if I already knew something wasn't right.

From the back she looked as if she'd just fallen asleep in her chair. I walked over, probably talking nonsense, but when I got to Nan, I could tell something was wrong.

'Nan?' I touched her on the shoulder, and she didn't move. Her face was all droopy on one side, expressionless, and I couldn't tell if she was awake or not. 'Nan!'

I ran back inside, panicking. My feet slapped the ground and my heart was pounding, but I knew what I had to do. The phone was one of those white plastic ones, a rectangle console and a handset that nestled in it, connected with a curly grey cord. I reckon every kid born in the '90s remembers those phones.

I dialed triple zero, waiting for the ringing sound. It was ironic, because Troy and I used to mess around on the phone all the time, prank calling triple zero. We were just kids – we didn't know any better – but I had a terrible, sinking feeling in my gut. What if they didn't take me seriously now when I really needed help?

Finally the operator answered the call and the sound of their voice gave me a rush of relief.

'My nan's sick! I don't know what's wrong with her, she isn't moving!' The rest of the conversation is a blur, but I must have given them our address.

I ran back to Nan. 'I'm going to Nanna Annabelle's, I'll be right back,' I told her, even though she wasn't showing any sign that she could hear me.

Nanna Annabelle lived few doors down from us, and I ran over, banging on the screen door. 'Nanna Annabelle! Nan's sick!'

Everything happened quickly. Nana Annabelle came rushing over to our house with me, badgering me with questions I couldn't answer. It felt as if the world was rushing around me in fast motion. People started appearing from everywhere, but I don't remember Mum being there at all. And Nan was still unresponsive in her chair, her face slack on one side. I couldn't bear to look at her. It felt so strange to see her like that.

The ambulance came, and the paramedics couldn't work out how to lift Nan out of her chair, so they just picked the whole thing up, with her still sitting in it, and moved it inside the van. She was a big woman by then, so tall and heavy-set in her old age, so it took some doing. Then they drove away, taking Nan to the hospital in Perth, nine hours away. Carnarvon Hospital didn't have the level of care that Nan needed.

I didn't know it then, but I would never see my nan as she used to be, ever again. I wish I could remember the last time we'd spent together before her stroke – whether we'd had a yarn, or played cards, or if she'd just called out to me: 'Brookey, come sit with your nan.' I wish I could bottle up the way she made me feel, as if I was the most special person in the world. She and I had a special connection – she gave me my totem, the sea turtle, and she was deeply connected to the ocean herself, the same as Mum – and me. We three women had the sea running through us.

In that Carnarvon house, the sea so close to us, enough to make the soil of our backyard sandy, we were tethered to the water. Nan was truly herself there in that backyard, tending to her little patch of soil, breathing in the eucalyptus soaked air, the salt of the sea adding an extra flavour to it.

But I don't have those memories. I swear, I would do anything to find a way back to them. And just like that, Nan was gone from the house, and she would never be back again. I don't remember when Mum finally showed up and found out what had happened, but she would have been gutted – absolutely wrecked that her mother had suffered and had been taken away, and that she wasn't there.

A few weeks passed in a haze, with news coming back from the hospital in Perth every few days about how Nan was doing. I was desperate to go and see her, but it was such a long drive. Finally, a few weeks after Nan had her stroke, Mum and Dragan packed us all up in the Commodore and set we off on the big drive south – Mum driving, Dragan next to her, and Troy, Eden and me squeezed into the back seat with RJ, only a toddler, in his car seat taking up another spot. We often drove like this, bending the rules and finding a way to fit an extra body into the car when we needed to.

Mum was frantic, but she still played her tunes on the way down. She loved hip hop and R'n'B, but then she also liked more alternative music; trance like God's Kitchen. The nine-hour drive was tense, and tedious. We often did that drive from Carnarvon to Perth – to see mob, and Dad lived in Perth too, so I was well used to the distance when I went to stay with him – but it didn't make it any less boring, and between that and worrying about Nan, it wasn't a fun trip at all. When we finally got to Perth, we went to Aunty Brenda's house in Kalamunda, on the eastern outskirts of the city. Her house was pretty swish, and despite being sad about Nan, Troy and I still made time to appreciate the trampoline in her backyard.

Then we went to visit Nan at the Royal Perth Hospital. I can almost feel the clinical smell hitting the back of my throat again – acidic and sharp, leaving a bad taste in my mouth. Nan was in a room on her own, lying on a bed, as still as can be, with cannulas and tubes everywhere and machine after machine connected to her. She just looked completely out of place, and her ring and her watch – which she always wore as a point of pride – weren't on her hands; they were tucked away in a little purse on the bedside table.

There were so many of us in that room – we probably caused a bit of a stir in the hospital, having the whole family come visit in one go. I don't know how lucid Nan was – the stress and grief of that visit have wiped out a lot of those memories – but I remember one special moment, just when we were leaving.

Nan reached out for me. 'Brookey,' she said, her voice faint. Mum moved out of the chair next to her bed, and I sat down. For as long as that moment was, it felt as if time had stopped, as if it was just the two of us and no one else in the room. I held Nan's hand, and I felt tears running down my cheeks. Even though I was hopeful she would get better, I think I knew that this was goodbye.

When we left, I was reluctant to let her hand go, crying because it felt so wrong to leave her there.

We drove home to Carnarvon soon after, and the house felt so strange without Nan. She brought a warmth and a level of care for us kids that was completely gone in her absence. Things didn't feel right. Mum wasn't coping. She was back on the drugs and edgier than usual, volatile, not sleeping, and not taking care of herself.

I tried to look after RJ, to make sure he was OK, and Troy and I fended for ourselves as we always did. Eden was still living with Susette, and Ky was in and out, the way she always was.

Soon it was RJ's birthday, and I was determined to make it special even though there was so much sadness in our house. My little brother would be turning three, and I wanted him to have a birthday cake for the occasion.

Birthdays were always a special thing for me. While they weren't celebrated at home with Mum, when I went to stay with Dad and Leanne, they always made a fuss when birthdays came around. At Dad's house, even though things weren't always great, birthdays and Christmas were happy times. He and Leanne were working class, but they had more money than we did, and their lives looked more 'normal', compared to what it was like living with Mum.

Their house was clean and neat, I had a comfortable bed to sleep in all to myself when I was there – and on my birthday I got cake and presents. Dad wouldn't ever let me take my presents back home with me when I left, probably because he didn't have positive feelings about Mum and our home, and because he wanted to keep them nice and safe at his place so I could enjoy them the next time I was there. I find it really interesting, though, that Mum always made sure I was dropped off to Dad for my birthday, and often for Christmas. Now I wonder if she did it because she knew I'd be spoiled there, with cake and gifts. Perhaps she did it because she knew she couldn't give me those things, but in her own way she wanted those occasions to be special.

If we were at home with Mum, a birthday was much like any other day. Even Christmas was pretty average – I remember one year, she clearly forgot about it, and must have dashed to the servo in Carnarvon the night before, grabbing whatever they had on sale. We got cheap snorkel gear that year – flippers and masks – wrapped in newspaper. It was hard not to feel a little disappointed when we saw the presents. I knew my friends and even my cousins would be bragging about their hauls later. But I also felt kind of sad, imagining Mum trying to find something decent with no money to spend and feeling terrible about running so late.

'Let's go to the blowholes!' she declared later, and that made up for it. It was a good Christmas in the end, us kids christening our snorkel gear in the clear water, and Mum lazing on the beach, in her element. Our celebrations as a family with Mum weren't typical, and sometimes they were downright sad, but we always made the most of what we had.

When RJ's birthday came around, I really wanted to make him a cake. There was so much that wasn't right – Nan was in hospital, Mum was using again, Bubba Shane had been taken away – and I just wanted one thing to celebrate.

Somehow, I got my hands on a $2 Black & Gold cake mix, and I figured I'd bake a cake for RJ and we could sing Happy Birthday to him, then eat it together. I was in the kitchen, working out the ingredients I needed to make the cake, when I saw Mum heading for the door.

'Hey, Mum! Where ya going?' I ran after her.

She was heading for the Commodore.

'What are you doing, Mum?'

'Going to see your nan,' she said shortly. She didn't seem like herself.

'But we just saw her,' I said. I was confused. We'd only come back from Perth a few days earlier, and it was a bloody long drive to go again so soon. Something seemed off – usually she and Dragan would go out together, or she'd take one of us kids, RJ usually.

'I'm going, I'll be back soon,' Mum said, obviously not in the mood to talk about it.

'But that's not fair,' I whined. 'It's RJ's birthday! And I want to come, I want to see Nan again!'

'You can't, Brooke.'

'Why not? Nan would want to see me! Why can't we go tomorrow, after we have RJ's birthday?'

Mum yelled at me. She didn't have a lot of patience at the best of times, and that day she looked like she was coming down. To me it also seemed as though things weren't good in her head.

She climbed into the car, turned the engine on and started backing down the driveway.

'I hate you!' I screamed, crying now. I was mad at her for leaving, and mad that I couldn't go and see Nan too. 'I hate you so much!'

Mum didn't stop, she didn't flinch. She just put the car in gear and accelerated down the road. I could see the outline of her through the rear window.

We didn't have anything I needed for the cake at our house. I took the cake mix over to Nanna Annabelle's, tears still streaking my cheeks, and she helped me make it. There, we somehow managed to have a little party for RJ. He was so excited, his little face lighting up when he understood the cake was for him, his little hands pushing cake into his mouth, smearing icing all over his cheeks.

Later, after RJ's party, we were all falling asleep in bed, when the worst happened. The house was dark, but the TV was on, and suddenly I heard commotion. I came out of the bedroom to find Ky and her boyfriend, Shane, and his family in the loungeroom.

Mum had an accident, they told us. She was gone. They'd come as soon as they'd heard.

I remember the overhead fluorescent lights flickering, and everything kind of rushing away from me in that moment. Nothing would ever be OK again.

For years, I thought that Mum had accidentally driven off the road. Lots of people die on the highways. It's probably the most dangerous thing we all do, and we barely think twice about it – we just climb into fast-moving metal cans and off we go down the road, no worries. But it's so easy for something to go wrong. It only takes the slightest mistake or the briefest lapse in concentration for you to end up hurt, or even dead.

So it wasn't crazy for me to think Mum's car had gone off the road and smashed into something – she could have been high or drunk, and she was also doing a nine-hour drive by herself. Years later, I would find out that she'd hit another car head-on, a man towing a caravan, who was also killed.

But for a long time afterwards, there was something that niggled away at me, something that made me think that perhaps it wasn't the whole story. Mum could be erratic, and make strange decisions. She ran hot, and she was impulsive, and her addiction definitely clouded her thinking. But it never made sense to me why she would just up and leave to drive back to Perth so soon after we'd come home. And why had she insisted on going by herself? She knew how close Nan and I were. Why wouldn't she have taken me with her?

Leaving on RJ's birthday was odd too. Mum loved her kids and she adored her baby, so why would she leave on his birthday, when she could just as easily have gone the next day?

It wasn't until years later, when I was talking to Grandma Susette, who gave me more context about how Mum was at that time, that I found out more about the way she died. Along with the rest of my my family, I now believe that Mum took her own life that night, driving between Carnarvon and Perth. It was incredibly hard for me to hear this at the time, but over the years I've come to understand it a bit better, and the initial anger I felt at Mum for making that choice has faded into more of a deep sadness.

You see, Mum and Nan had a special kind of bond. They were inseparable.

They certainly fought and argued and butted heads. But they were more than just mother and daughter, they were tethered to each other in another way altogether. I remember talking to my Uncle Pete about Nan and Mum's relationship, and he told me that Nan had always wanted to keep Mum close to her.

'From the moment Seanna was born, Charlotte didn't want to let her go,' he said. Even though Nan had many siblings, and had five children, and had loved and lost different men in her lifetime, once Seanna had grown up, she found herself mostly alone.

When Mum fell pregnant at sixteen, Nan said to her, 'That's it. Now you'll live with me, and we'll take care of the baby together.' Now, I don't think Mum ever regretted having Ky, or the rest of us, but she definitely had goals in her youth.

Even though school wasn't always her priority, she was a bright spark, and she had plans to enrol in a counselling course. Falling pregnant at such a young age changed all that, and I reckon there were many things Mum could have done if she'd had different options or advice back then, if she'd been told it was her choice whether she kept the baby or not.

But from that moment, her life was set on a particular course, and over the years, the balance of Mum and Nan's relationship swung back and forth. Nan needed Mum, and us kids, because we gave her family and a purpose, and people to care for and to be cared by.

But equally, as Mum's addiction took hold, as she had five kids and rocketed between partners, and houses, and hand-to-mouth jobs, Nan was a constant presence. Mum knew that if Nan was there, her kids were safe and cared for. She knew that what she couldn't give us herself, Nan could. Nan gave us stories and hugs, routine and life lessons, and a connection to our culture and country. I'm sure Mum wanted to be able to do those things for us, but she was so weighed down by her own demons, it never felt possible.

They each gave the other something important and vital.

Seeing Nan so helpless in hospital would have been confronting as all hell for Mum. Charlotte was such a strong, powerful force in Seanna's life, I think she was shocked to the core by the fact that that her mum could die, and that she'd have to step into her shoes and be the matriarch herself. I don't think she was ready for it.

I also think Mum scared herself sometimes. I think she was afraid of what would happen to us without Nan, because she didn't trust herself to care for us, to keep us safe and out of the system. I think Mum drove away from me that day, my shouts still ringing in her ears, knowing she wasn't coming back. I think she did it because she thought it would set us free, force us all out of the negative cycles we were caught in. She knew that without her and Nan in the picture, we'd be split up – and that perhaps it would be better that way.

Mum took her own life. I wish so much that she hadn't, but I now see how much pressure and grief she was feeling. She thought she was doing us all a favour.

Suicide is such a taboo subject for so many of us. I've worked in mental health for long enough to know that what drives someone to that place is more complicated than we sometimes realise. When I first heard from Grandma Susette that Mum crashed her car on purpose that night, I was angry. I felt that she'd taken the easy way out. I wished I could go back in time and yell at her to snap out of it, that leaving for us was nowhere near as good as staying for us. That we needed her. That we loved her.

Now, I have a different view, and I feel such intense sadness. I love my mum just as fiercely now as I did then, and what makes me fill up with grief is wondering whether she knew how loved she was, how much we all adored her. I think Mum felt like a shitty parent most of the time, and that she battled constantly with her demons. I swear to God if I could meet her now, I'd tell her that in the eyes of her children she was a hero.

Whenever Mum's Commodore pulled up at the front of the house, us kids ran outside to greet her as if she was a pop star or a celebrity. She was our Janet Jackson, stylish in her jeans and T-shirt, her hair in wild waves around her beautiful face, charisma oozing out of her. She was like a light that drew us all in around her, like moths to a flame.

When she was well, and could laugh and joke with us, and pack us into the car for a trip to the ocean or find a few bucks to shout us ice creams, we felt so happy we could burst. Whenever I saw her from a distance – when she was waiting outside the school or walking back to us on the beach after having a swim – I'd think, *That's my mum*, and I'd fill up with pride.

Mum was fierce. She had a really strong sense of justice. She didn't always do things the way she knew she should – she had a very quick temper, and she could be unpredictable, especially when she was using – but I know that if she'd had different opportunities or options in life, she would have set the whole world alight with her passion and her ambition and her abilities. She was just an absolute ripper. A matriarch in her own right. A proud blak woman who raised me to be a proud blak woman, too.

What I wouldn't give to have her back, but I lost her, and I truly believe that the world lost someone remarkable that night.

A lot of what I remember about the night that Mum died is feeling like the world was slipping away from under me, like I was in freefall. Some details are clear though, like Aunty Brenda stepping in to organise everything; getting Mum's body identified and transported back to Carnarvon for the funeral. I still wonder if anyone told Nan in the hospital in Perth. She was barely conscious. I can't imagine what her grief would have been to know that her beautiful Seanna was gone, and that her grandkids were suffering without their nan to comfort them.

I'm really grateful that Aunty Brenda took on the huge mental and emotional task of organising Mum's funeral, though it was hard for us kids because we didn't get to have a say in what happened, and Nan wasn't there to step in for us. The strange thing is that, even though Mum was so young when she died – only thirty-four – we actually knew quite a bit of what she wanted for her funeral and her final resting place. We knew she wanted to be buried in Quairading on her mother's country – and we even knew which song she wanted played at her funeral, which, looking back, could have been a warning sign.

I have a very clear memory from the house in Carnarvon when we were quite young, and Mum was blasting Akon's 'Mama Africa' on Eden's sound system in his room – we would play music so loud on that stereo that you could hear it through the whole house. That stereo was one of the many contradictions in our lives then – for instance, we didn't have food in the fridge, but we had a stereo and CDs. We even had a computer for a while, and Mum would burn CDs on it, but we never had new clothes or other necessities. Sometimes we had a packet of A4 printing paper in the house, which was like gold to me as a kid, and I could use it to draw or make crafts ... but we didn't have lunch money. It was confusing.

On this particular day, Mum was in a reflective mood, and we were lounging around, listening to the music. Then, out of nowhere, she told us, 'When I die, I want "Purple Rain" by Prince played at my funeral.'

'Don't be silly Mum, you're not gonna die,' I said, laughing. I thought she was playing around – to me it seemed impossible that my mum could die.

'"Purple Rain",' she repeated firmly. 'You kids remember that.'

We told Aunty Brenda, but she was so busy organising the funeral it wasn't included in the playlist, and the songs that were played are all ruined for me now – I can't hear them without feeling a jolt of stress and sadness.

Now, as an adult, I've been to more funerals than I've been to weddings, but Mum's funeral was my first. It was at the Church of Christ in Carnarvon, and us kids were the last people to walk in. There were seats for us at the very front of the church, and we had to walk past everyone to get there.

I felt numb that day. I was trying to keep an eye on RJ and Troy, but I could barely concentrate. It was a closed casket, and I'm so glad for that now, that my memories of Mum are only of when she was alive, and not of her body without her spirit in it. None of us kids spoke at the funeral – we were all just too wiped out with our grief.

People kept coming up to us and telling us they were sorry, hugging us. We all left the church following the casket, as the pallbearers carried Mum out to the hearse. Then we were driven behind the hearse to the Carnarvon cemetery, where Mum would be buried, which has always made us sad, because she wasn't laid to rest where she'd wanted, on Noongar country, next to Nan's parents and siblings. Once the casket was lowered into the grave, we each came forward to throw a handful of dirt onto it. I couldn't make sense of it, that my mother was in that box, and was about to be buried in dirt. I consoled Troy, who was sobbing, and tried to give him strength even though I felt like collapsing from the weight of my own grief.

Afterwards we went back to our house for the wake. Being the middle of May, it was starting to get cold and there were big old oil drums set up for bonfires in the backyard. There were lots of platters of food, which everyone there had contributed to, and someone had found us an urn for tea and coffee. And of course there was booze.

Before long, the adults were getting pissed, yarning about Mum, their grief moving from tears to laughter at some memory or another. There were lots of people there, and I remember trying to keep an eye on the kids, my brothers and cousins, which was often the role I played at the parties Mum would throw.

As the night wore on, the place started getting more crowded, so I eventually gathered the kids up and took them to Nanna Annabelle's house next door. I got everyone settled in the lounge with blankets and cushions and whatever else I could find. I made sure they'd all had something to eat, and checked on my brothers, to make sure were OK.

And then, for some reason, I went back home. I wanted to sleep in my own bed, I think. Without Mum and Nan there, I just felt lost. I wanted something familiar. I climbed into my bed, and shut my eyes, and tried to sink into darkness so I could escape this awful day.

This next thing is hard to write.

I'm conflicted about it, because it was the catalyst for the next few stages of my life, and perhaps in some twisted way, it was the trigger that set me on the path that ultimately led to me to where I am now. But it was also the worst, the ugliest, most traumatic thing that happened to me, when I was just a child.

I went to sleep, and when I woke up, I was aware that I was being assaulted. I don't want to write the details, and to be honest, a lot of it has been blanked out in my memory, my brain trying to protect me.

But I remember it being the early hours of the morning, before dawn, and that I was terrified. I remember that when it was over, somehow I got myself to Nanna Annabelle's house. Did I walk or run there? Did I get dressed, did I get shoes on my feet? Did anyone see me leave? I don't have the answers to any of these questions.

At Nanna Annabelle's, I found the phone in the kitchen, and a phone book. I remember searching under my father's last name and his address. I dialled the number.

'Hello?'

'Dad? It's me, Brooke.'

'Brooke? What are you calling so early for?'

'Dad, something happened.'

I tried to find the words to tell him what had happened, but I couldn't. I didn't have the language, and I knew what might happen to me if I told anyone – I'd end up in another foster home. I eleven years old. All I asked was that he come and get me.

In the background, I could hear Leanne saying, 'You need to go and get her.'

'I'll come now, Brooke,' Dad said. 'You get your things and sit tight.'

I went back home, and I found one of those plastic storage bags that you can buy at the $2 shop, the ones that are chequered all over. I stuffed clothes and shoes and other bits and pieces into the bag, and then I sat and waited.

It's a nine-hour drive from Perth to Carnarvon, and how those hours passed I have no idea. I didn't tell anyone what had happened, or explain where I was going, but Aunty Katrina or Nana Annabelle must have known that Dad was coming to get me.

And then, finally, Dad was there, and we were in the car, heading to a whole new life that I had no idea was coming my way.

I'm grateful that he came to collect me. It's one of the few moments in my life when my father behaved in a way that showed that, on some level, he cared about me. But the nine hours in the car with him weren't easy. I was in shock, and I remember Dad trying to make conversation, even getting a little annoyed at me for not chatting. We ate McDonald's on the road, and even while I was numb from shock and trauma and grief, I still registered that it was exciting to be eating McDonald's, which was always such a major treat for us kids.

When we got to Perth, we went straight to my dad's parents' house, where Dad was living at the time. He and Leanne, his partner, were separated then, and he was staying there while he and Leanne worked things out. Going there first was unfortunate for me, because Grandma had never been kind to me. She hated Mum, and she'd never accepted me as part of the family. I always felt judged and disliked when I was around her.

Leanne was there too, and as they started talking, I slipped away to the bathroom. I went to the toilet, and seeing that there was blood in my underwear, I felt sick. I didn't fully understand why it was happening – I knew it was wrong, but I didn't want the adults to know anything about what had happened to me, so I took my underwear off and hid it at the bottom of the bathroom bin.

By the time I'd emerged, they'd made the decision that I'd go home with Leanne.

'She's just lost her mum. She needs a woman right now,' Leanne had said wearily.

I was relieved to be leaving my grandparents, but I was apprehensive, too, because I hadn't stayed with Leanne on my own before.

Leanne drove me to her place in Armadale, where my brothers from my dad's side lived too. In her bedroom, she set up a camper bed next to hers, and put my bag of belongings against the wall. I curled up on the camper bed, and finally let my body relax, the exhaustion of the past twenty-four hours finally hitting me.

My mind was still racing. In that moment of crisis, I had just followed my instinct to run. I needed to get away, I wanted to be safe, and I did what made sense to me. But now, so far away in Perth, I realised that I'd left my brothers on their own. Where would they go next? When would I see them again?

Ky and Eden were older, they could look after themselves. But Troy and RJ, at just eight and three years old, what would happen to them? I felt sick with anxiety, and I just wanted to bury myself under the covers and wake up to find out it was all just an awful nightmare, that Mum was on her way to pick me up as though this was a regular visit to Dad.

I wouldn't tell Dad or Leanne that I'd been assaulted until much later in my life, and eventually the impact of losing Mum and Nan, and the assault, would catch up with me.

But for now, I had launched myself forward, into a new life. At eleven years of age, I had seen more of the darker side of life than most kids my age, and the next chapter was going to either make or break me.

Four

I've been through a few major shifts in my life. Becoming one of Channel Ten's Bachelorettes comes to mind, but the move from everything that I knew and everyone I loved in Carnarvon to living full-time with Leanne was one of the most significant in my life.

It wasn't even the obvious things that felt strange. While I was grieving for Mum and dealing with the trauma of my assault, those deeper emotional wounds took a back seat to the practical things in the here and now in my child's life. For a start, I didn't love sleeping in Leanne's room on the camper bed, but the house she rented was a three-bedroom-one-bathroom, and Tye and Kallom each had a bedroom.

Bizarrely, my younger brothers on both sides mirrored each other in age. Tye, Leanne and Dad's eldest son, was almost the exact same age as Troy, and Kallom was only a few months younger than RJ. But that was where the similarities ended – Tye and Kallom didn't need me, or see me as a big sister in the way Troy and RJ did. It had also been quite a few months since I had spent any time with them.

That contrast made the separation from Troy and RJ harder. For a while, I didn't know where they were, though I eventually found out that Troy was staying with Grandma Susette in Perth, and RJ was with his father, Dragan, in Carnarvon. Eden was living with his dad in Onslow, and Ky was off being Ky.

In those first few weeks at Leanne's, I felt awkward and embarrassed that I'd needed Dad and Leanne to rescue me. I crept around the house, trying to stay out of the way as much as I could. Though he and Leanne were separated, Dad would stay there occasionally, but Leanne was very much the adult in charge of me. I tried my best to be easy to have in the house; I knew it was a big sacrifice on Leanne's part to be taking in her stepdaughter when she wasn't even with my father anymore, and he wasn't always around to help.

The worst thing about the whole situation was that Nan was in hospital, in the same city, and I couldn't go and see her.

'Please can we go to visit?' I'd ask Dad on the few occasions I saw him. But it seemed to me that he never had time, or the petrol cost too much.

And then, only a few weeks later, Nan passed away. I'll always remember Leanne finding me in the house and breaking the news. I cried my eyes out on the camper bed for hours.

It felt as if everyone I loved, everyone who loved me, was leaving me. The door was firmly shut now on my old life, because without Mum and Nan, my life in Carnarvon just didn't exist anymore. I was homesick, but it was for a memory now – the memory of being surrounded by my mob, my family, and the two strongest women I had ever known. Now they were gone, and that part of my life was lost forever. Lying there on that camper bed, I was grieving for far more than just my nan and my mum.

Nan's funeral was in Quairading, on her country. She was buried where her mother, father and siblings were.

'Do you have something black to wear?' Leanne asked before she drove me to the service.

'I'm not wearing black,' I said staunchly. 'Nan hated it. She'd want us wearing her favourite colours.'

I wore turquoise, which Nan loved – it reminded her of the ocean. Walking into the church in that colour, it felt right, as if I was honouring her memory.

I was so glad Leanne was there with me. As the only white woman at the funeral, she would have felt awkward, and I could tell she wasn't familiar with the ways of our sorry business, but even still, she came up to my family with me and gave her condolences.

Even with the sadness, I was so glad to see my brothers, and Ky. We huddled together, our little family that was so changed now without Mum and Nan to hold it together. Uncle Pinhead was there too. In the time that I'd been away, he'd landed in prison, but he'd been granted leave to attend his mother's funeral. He had two prison guards with him, and his ankles and wrists were chained, which meant I couldn't even hug him.

The church was small, but full of people who loved my nan, and I could hear the soft sound of her sisters weeping. As the congregation entered the church, they were filing past Nan's coffin to pay their respects. Hand in hand, Leanne and I joined the queue, only realising a moment too late that it was an open casket. Leanne tried to shield me from it, but we'd reached the top of the queue.

There was Nan, lying peacefully in the casket. She'd had make-up put on her, and it felt so wrong to see her like that. I wanted her to jump up, to call me 'Brookey' and tell me to come sit, for a yarn. I wanted the living, breathing Nan, not this shell of her body. I wish I could scrub that sight from my memory so I never have think of her like that again.

After the funeral, I didn't see my family again for a long time. When we went back to Leanne's house, I tried to square my shoulders and commit to this new life, even though it was hard to stop feeling like an imposter.

Living with Leanne took some getting used to, but of course it would have been hard for her to suddenly have a grieving, traumatised tween in her care. At the time she wasn't working and looking after us full time, and Dad was over sometimes, when he wasn't staying with his parents or at a caravan park. He was working on and off, mostly driving trucks, and he wasn't around enough to be much of a father figure to either me or to his sons. Every so often when he stayed at Leanne's, he'd park a big semi-trailer out the front of the house. If the tray was empty, Tye and Kallom and I would climb up there and use it like a stage, and put on performances. But in those first few weeks, I was very unsure of myself and had no idea how to be part of this new family.

The house was in Armadale, a fairly low socio-economic area south-west of Perth. Leanne kept it neat and tidy, and even little things, like having doors on the cupboards and the carpet being cleaned with a vacuum cleaner, made it feel more posh than anything I was used to. Another big difference was that there was always food in the pantry. Even as sad and as tired as I was, I was excited about that, though for a while I felt too awkward to just go and help myself.

Thankfully, when I arrived to live with Leanne, it was the middle of school term, and she got me enrolled in primary school straight away – I was relieved because it meant I didn't have to face too many days hanging around the house. Being eleven, that year was my last in primary school, and the following year I would need to move to yet another – high school. And God all mighty, I hated starting new schools! I did it often enough, so you'd think I would've been used to it, but it was just so exhausting being the new kid. You never knew what socially complicated relationships and power dynamics you were stepping into, and I dreaded working that stuff out and having to make new friends.

I felt sick to my stomach getting ready in my new uniform. Leanne drove Tye and me to school, and I remember wishing I could just go back in time to my old school in Carnarvon, with Skyla and Troy. It was ironic though, because in reality I never had much trouble making friends. It sounds arrogant to say this, but whenever I started a new school, other kids seemed to be drawn to me, and I always had someone actively approaching me, wanting to be my friend. Perhaps it's because I was athletic, and with my unusual skin tone, being part Indigenous and part Malaysian, even seemed a bit exotic to the suburban kids in Perth. I can't know for sure, but as always, despite all my nerves, I had new friends by lunchtime.

There was so much that was different about this city school, compared to the country school I went to in Carnarvon – for a start, there were just so many more kids. After my first couple of weeks, there was a sports carnival, which I was excited about. I entered as many of the sprints as I could – in Carnarvon my favourites were the 100, 200 and 400 metres – and with new kids to race against against it was good to feel a normal sense of competition, distracting me from my sadness.

No matter where I went, I always loved sport and I always wanted to win. To me there's nothing better than the freedom of sprinting in a race, adrenaline in your veins and your heart pumping in your chest and in your ears. After that carnival, I joined Little Athletics and the local netball team, which gave me my first ever group of girlfriends. I also joined the school choir, but because we couldn't afford the costumes, I just did all the practice and rehearsals, and sat out of the actual big performances. I'd later drop out anyway, because truth be told, I'm not the best singer!

I was so dislocated when I arrived at Leanne's that year. I had suffered so much loss so quickly, and I was still so young, I didn't know how to talk about my grief or trauma, let alone process it. So I compartmentalised it, throwing myself into all that activity at my new school. I deliberately kept Nan and Mum out of my thoughts as much as I could manage, and tried my hardest to push the rest of my family out of my mind when I could. That was easier said than done – there was nothing I could do about the terrible guilt I felt in the pit of my stomach when it came to my younger brothers.

It makes me so sad to think of that now, because I was so little – so young and lonely – and feeling as though I should carry the responsibility for them. Again, I must give credit to Leanne, who was doing her best for me, but she couldn't give me the complex emotional support I needed at the time – I was living with the burden of what had happened to me at Mum's wake on my own, so I coped by just trying to push past my sadness and survive.

After those initial few weeks, and with school putting me back into a routine, I started to settle into my new life. At first, I didn't speak unless I was spoken to, and I tried to make myself as small as possible, so as not to be noticed or become a burden.

After a while though, when I started to understand that I would be staying put for a bit, I started to loosen up a little – and the real Brooke started to emerge. And the real Brooke wasn't quite as shy and retiring as the grieving, quiet version of me that had arrived in Perth, especially at school.

Despite what had happened to me, I was actually a pretty strong spirit, with a very independent streak. And when I started hitting puberty and becoming a teenager, that meant I turned into a little bit of a shit-stirrer!

I remember being in scripture class that term, and challenging the teacher about how exactly Jesus had risen from the dead. Back in Carnarvon, we went to church a little bit – mostly when we were in foster care with Ken and Barb. They took us to Sunday School, which I loved, but I can't say I had much of an understanding of Jesus, God or the Bible. To me, Jesus was the reason why we did fun activities like craft and playing footy with other kids, and having a feed. As far as I cared, I loved Jesus! He was my mate!

But there in the classroom, being taught about how Jesus was born, how he died, and about the miracles he performed, made zero sense to me. I listened for a bit, but then I couldn't help it. I had to put my hand up.

'Hang on, so you're telling me this guy came out of nowhere, his dad is God, and he can come back from the dead?' I asked sceptically. Every head in the classroom swivelled my way, and let's just say, the teacher was not impressed.

I was always quite independent and individual at school. My first 'boyfriend' is another good example of this, because no one would have paired us together in their wildest dreams. If I was becoming one of the cool kids, Riley was right at the other end of the spectrum. My core memory of Riley is that he used to pick his nose and eat it. Everyone thought he was gross. But I kind of liked him. He marched to the beat of his own drum, and I respected that. We got to know each other, and then we became 'boyfriend' and 'girlfriend', which in primary school meant that we just held hands for a while.

Other kids were confused by it. 'Why would you want to hang out with Riley?' they'd ask.

I'd shrug. 'He's cool,' I'd say. Judging people made no sense to me – growing up I'd already seen so much dysfunction that some kid picking his nose felt like a very trivial thing to have an opinion on. I always had a soft spot for the underdog as well – for my whole life, people had made assumptions about me, about my mum, about our family, our culture. They dismissed us because we were blak and poor, and they got us wrong every time. I wasn't interested in doing the same thing; I wanted to take people for who they were.

Those last few months of primary school passed calmly for me. There were so many reasons for the other kids to judge me or treat me badly at school – I was the new kid, Indigenous, poor, and I didn't have the same kind of family life as most kids. But I never once felt like an outsider, which made all the difference to me arriving in Armadale.

Before long it was time for graduation. I knew that everyone would be wearing fancy clothes to our ceremony, and I was feeling a bit panicky about what I would wear. I didn't have much when it came to a wardrobe, and what I did have was pretty practical – my school uniform, sport gear like shorts and T-shirts, only a few casual bits and pieces that I'd brought with me from Carnarvon, and necessities from Leanne.

'I'll take you shopping, but you're going to have to save up,' Leanne told me, when I asked if I could get a new dress.

So she set me chores, and I'd vacuum or tidy the house for a few bucks here and there. We went to the local Westfields shopping complex together – The Carousel – and I found a beautiful purple dress that I absolutely loved. It was about $50, and Leanne kicked in the rest to get it for me.

While Leanne could be a little strict, she was there for me in ways that no parent had been in my life up to then.

She wasn't the kind of person to give me a kiss on the forehead, but I'd always get a packed lunch. Life with her was reliable and her house was comfortable – I knew I'd be fed, showered and warm in bed – but I'd leapt from having very little supervision to suddenly having constant supervision, someone who was always checking on me, wanting to know where I was, what I ate, whether I'd had a shower, when I woke up. These are normal things that most parents demand of their children, but I'd never had that before, and it took some getting used to. I was still so conscious of being there, too, that sometimes that I felt like a nuisance or a burden.

Leanne was doing her best to care for me, but I always felt anxious because there were expectations of me I'd never had before, and I didn't quite understand where they were coming from. My arrival was a really big shake-up in both our lives, and a lot of the time we were just trying to work each other out, but it's testament to the life I was living with Leanne that I started calling her 'Mum' by the end of that year.

Ultimately, our relationship would flare when I was in high school, but in the meantime life was calm and ordered and I began to let out the breath I'd been holding in since Mum died.

Over the summer, I found a new best friend. Sam (Samantha) lived across the road from us in Armadale, and her mum and Leanne were best mates. Sam was a year younger than me, but that didn't make any difference to us, and we hung out every minute we could.

We did all the usual tween-girl things – lying on her bed listening to music, going for walks, making up games. In some ways, Sam was probably the first girl I had feelings for that went beyond friendship. She was special to me, not in the same way that my previous close female friends like Skyla had been. But at that age, it was easy to push those feelings aside.

Sam's mum gave us both our first after-school jobs. She worked for a company sorting and folding advertising mailouts – junk mail – and Sam and I would ride around the neighbourhood on our pushbikes, delivering the catalogues. We'd spend hours at Sam's house, carefully folding the brochures into neat rectangles; then we'd stuff them into plastic bags and head off, one bag balanced on each handle of our bikes. I loved that job – I don't know if it was the peacefulness of doing something repetitive and precise like folding the catalogues, or the freedom of riding my bike through the streets with Sam, but I remember those summer afternoons with so much fondness.

By now I had my own room. Kallom, who was only a preschooler, moved in with Leanne so I could have his old room, and I still feel so grateful to Leanne for trying to give me what I needed at that time. She knew that as an almost-teenager, I needed some privacy and a space of my own. The last time I had my own bedroom was with Ken and Barb, in foster care.

I loved having a room to myself, but Leanne had decorated it for me, and let's just say that we didn't really see eye to eye when it came to décor! Walking into my bedroom was like entering a shrine to all things girly: there was pink everywhere – the walls, the bedspread, the pillows. I was never a 'girly girl', and I say that with the full knowledge that gender identity is so much more complex than being 'girly' or 'macho'. But in the early 2000s, gender culture was still pretty binary, and I knew even then I wasn't a typical girl.

For Leanne, though, who didn't have a daughter of her own, it would have been so special to turn that bedroom into what she thought I would like. She'd also seen me growing up with Mum, missing out on so many of the things that most kids take for granted, like birthday presents and cakes, and witnessed the times when Mum dealt with normal childhood issues in extreme ways, like shaving our heads because we kept getting nits.

I had nits so many times as a kid, I can't even count. They were a constant plague, and I have many memories of Nan working through my hair after treating it with medicated shampoo. I'd be sitting on the ground in front of her in her chair in the backyard as she pulled the fine toothed comb through my wet hair; then she'd flick the nits onto the ground in front of us. If she caught one on its own, she'd crack it in half with her fingernails, and I'd shudder. It was awful.

Once, I was sitting in class when I felt a nit crawl across my forehead. Other kids saw it, and everyone squealed and told me how disgusting it was, laughing at me. I still shrivel inside with shame when I think about that – it's one of my standout memories of growing up poor, and being judged for it. It was hard for us to get rid of the nits because of how we lived, sharing

85

beds with multiple kids, and not having enough money for the treatment all the time. Eventually Mum got sick of the constant battle, so she shaved our heads. The next time I saw Dad and Leanne, they were horrified; people thought I was a boy, and I remember being dressed in pink.

But the truth is, I didn't really care about having my hair shaved off, or people thinking I was a boy. I was just never that interested in traditionally feminine things.

So, while it was wonderful to have a room of my own, it was so pink that it didn't ever really feel as if it was completely my space. Perhaps the worst thing about it was the wallpaper. Back then it was quite popular to wallpaper halfway down the room and paint the bottom half a feature colour. The wallpaper on my room had bunny cartoons on it, and maths equations – and infuriatingly, the maths was wrong! The bunnies looked very pleased with themselves next to a problem that had two carrots plus two carrots as equalling five. And every time I looked at them, I'd want to yell 'It's four, you morons!' Not to mention suffering the laughter of my friends as they pointed out the mistake.

But complaints aside, I treasured that bedroom for the privacy it gave me, though one of the contradictions was that it took me a while to feel safe sleeping on my own – when I arrived to live with Leanne I was plagued with nightmares of the assault and knowing she was right beside me in her bedroom was a big comfort.

Leanne found me a beautiful dresser with a round mirror on it, and I laid out all my toiletries on it, displayed elegantly so you could see each individual bottle and jar, like perfume and sweet-smelling moisturisers. I'd even display the empty bottles, just because I liked how pretty they looked. I'd never had toiletries before that were mine and mine alone, and it was exciting to have somewhere to put things that I knew would stay where I left them.

Pretty soon, I was about to start high school – Year 8. (Until 2015, the high school system in Western Australia started in Year 8 and finished in Year 12.) For the first time in my young life I had a significant decision to make, one that would shape the next five years of my life – which school?

At the end of primary school, a representative from one of the local high schools came and talked our year about their football program as a way of encouraging kids to come to the school. By then, I'd already made a name for myself as a sporty, competitive kid, and had been doing really well in the netball team I was playing for, playing centre and wing attack, and at Little Athletics I was particularly good at sprinting, and javelin and discus. Javelin and discus may seem like random sports to have a natural talent for, but any Koori kids who've grown up in the country will know that throwing rocks is one of our all-time favourite pastimes.

Back in Carnarvon, we used to throw 'bundis' all the time. Bundis are what we call sand that's been compacted together into a loose rock, which smashes when it hits something. Is there anything more satisfying than throwing a bundi and seeing it blast apart when it hits your target?

'Bet I can hit that stop sign!' Troy would say, and then we'd both have a go, grabbing rocks or bundis from the ground.

Years later, when I was working in remote communities in the Northern Territory, the kids out there were just the same.

'Hey, bet I can throw my rock all the way to that tree!' one of them would shout. And the next minute, they'd all be having a go. Even recently, when I was on a trip with a mate, and we were waiting for a car in a country area, I found myself bending down to grab a nice, hefty rock, and then gestured at a sign a way off down the road.

'Wanna see if I can hit that?' I asked. I reckon I was just as stoked to hit that sign as I would have been as a kid.

Of course, there's a kind of sense to it, because mob have hunted with rocks throughout time. It was one of the most common ways to get food, to use rocks to hunt goanna, and other slower-moving prey, so perhaps there's a hereditary element to it too. But whatever the case, all that practice chucking bundis meant by the time I had to throw a discus for the first time, I had a pretty good aim and strength, and the same with javelin.

As for the sprinting, I'd always loved running as a kid.

'I'll race ya!' I'd yell to Troy, whenever we were heading to the milk bar for lollies, or even just on our way to school. Why walk when you can run? Running made me feel free – but even more exhilarating than the physical liberation of running was winning. I *loved* winning. I loved knowing that I was good at it, and that I could beat everyone else, leave them in my dust.

I'm a competitive person, but not because I need to be better than everyone. I think it's more about having something that no one can take away. Whether or not I won a race came down to me and me alone – my body, my mind, and what I could do with both was up to me. I never felt as alive as when I took that final step over the finish line, the adrenaline pumping through me, knowing I was the winner.

When the representative from the local public high school, Cecil Andrews College, came to talk to us, he told us that they were starting an AFL program for girls and boys, and that anyone was welcome to join. The idea of playing AFL made me sit up and pay attention. One of my all-time favourite pastimes back home with Nan had been watching the footy on telly – without fail she could name every Indigenous player across the entire league, and I looked up to them, especially her Fremantle favourites, Jeff Farmer, and Troy Cook, who I know as Uncle Troy. Apparently he used to change my nappies when I was a baby! Mum and Nan would have loud arguments about who would win the league – Nan was a rusted on Dockers fan and Mum's team was the Essendon Bombers.

Playing footy was just part of my everyday life, too, playing long ranging games through the streets with my brothers and cousins, and in the summer before Mum died, I'd even played some games with the local club.

The only problem was that I'd already applied to a private girls school, St Brigid's College, and had been offered a scholarship for their netball program. A representative from St Brigid's had also come and spoken to our year, and all my friends in the netball team said they were applying for the program, so I did too.

Leanne helped me with the application, and we were excited to have won a scholarship, but I remember we were both a bit daunted by the prospect of enrolling there. The school was almost an hour away in Lesmurdie by car or by bus, and financially it was a big commitment – while the netball scholarship paid for my tuition, it didn't cover the uniform or any other costs. And it was posh; the school looked like a fancy hotel to me – so different to what I was used to. I felt intimidated just thinking about it.

On the other hand, Cecil Andrews College had footy, most of my friends would go there, and I could walk there from home.

I was a teenager, and every extra minute of sleep was precious to me. I chose the school within walking distance!

High school was another big transition for me. Even though I'd experienced so much in my short life up until then, I was still quite naive, and didn't have an older sibling to guide me in the ways of high school. When the bell rang at the end of my very first class, I watched, confused, as everyone got up and started gathering their things to leave. I figured it was just like primary school, where we stayed in one room all day. It wasn't until the teacher was leaving that she noticed me still sitting there.

'You OK, honey?' she asked. 'What class do you have next?'

'Society and Environment,' I said, double-checking my timetable.

'OK – do you know where it is?'

'Isn't it here?'

Thanks to that teacher, I made it to my next class on time, and by the end of the first week I'd worked it all out for the most part. But high school opened me up to a totally different side of life. I was starting to figure out who I was, and with that came some changes to my attitude, too. For the first time, I started to care about how I looked. I would wake up really early in the morning so I could get ready for school, and part of that was straightening my hair with one of those thin Remington hair straighteners that I reckon every girl had in the early 2000s.

Then I'd iron my school skirt – some habits die hard, because just like in Carnarvon, I wanted my uniform to look exactly like everyone else's. Leanne didn't like how hard I was trying to fit in; she just wanted me to be myself, and she'd stop by my bedroom sometimes, watch me fussing over my hair, and say, 'You don't have to do all that, you know?' But I wanted to. My school photo from my first year of high school shows a little girl with carefully brushed hair with a green bow in it, smiling innocently at the camera in a sort of shy, hesitant way.

Fast forward to the following year, and the carefully primped look is gone, and I've got an edgy mullet vibe happening. By Year 11, it was full-blown punk hair and a lip ring.

With the benefit of hindsight, I can see that I wasn't always the easiest student – I could be mouthy and talk back, but I think deep down my teachers knew I was a good kid, and they wanted me to succeed; some of them could probably tell that I hadn't had the easiest path in life. Sometimes the weight of what I'd been through would get on top of me, and the anxiety was so bad that I'd tell Leanne I wasn't feeling well – bad period pain or a phantom cold – and I'd miss school, up to days at a time.

I was conflicted, because a big part of me really wanted to do well at school. I still wanted to be a good role model for Troy and RJ and make them proud. I wanted them to see that there was a different path in life from the one Mum had taken, and the one that Ky was taking. Being so young, I couldn't connect all the dots in my logic, but naively, I thought that if I did well, I could show them the value of education, and maybe they could have a different life too.

It was around this time that I made a pact with myself not to have sex until I was sixteen. That was how old Ky was when she had Bubba Shane, and how old Mum was when she had Ky, and it was also how old Nan was when she had her first baby, so to me that age felt like destiny or fate for the women in my family. I vowed that no matter what, it would not happen to me.

Another goal I made was that I wanted to stay at the same school for the entirety of high school. Again, I hadn't connected all the dots as I was regularly absent, but I'd been moved around to so many schools that I was behind academically as a result. While I knew clearly that education was something that could change my life, it was also in real danger of slipping away if I kept the same pattern, so it was important to me that I finished high school at the same place.

And because I'm not one to shy away from a lofty ambition, I also decided I wanted to finish high school as Head Girl in Year 12. That seemed like the kind of achievement that would prove I was going places, something Troy and RJ could really look up to. I wasn't sure how I was going to get there, but I remember seeing the plaque outside the teachers' lounge with the names of past Head Boys and Girls engraved on it and decided my name would be there one day, too.

As it happened, I would end up spending quite a bit of time in the teachers' lounge, because that was where I first met Jo. Of all the many people who have played an important role in my life, Jo is perhaps the most significant. I didn't know it when I first met her, but she changed my life.

At our first meeting, Jo was a gruff, middle-aged teacher who ran the 'Follow the Dream' program for Aboriginal kids at the school. She was really no-nonsense in the way she dressed and spoke, always in jeans and a comfortable T-shirt or jumper, her hair short and her attitude very straight to the point. There was a warmth to Jo that I felt immediately, even when I barely knew her.

Follow the Dream was an after-school program, where we were tutored and given help with our homework. There were other resources too – we talked about our options after school in terms of future study, work and careers, and we spent time with teachers and mentors who could help us with the problems that our classroom teachers didn't always have the time for. Best of all, we got a free feed! Again, some habits die hard.

From the moment I met Jo, I felt a strong connection to her. She always showed an interest in me and my life – for me, she was a safe person from the get-go. I knew she didn't have kids, and that she lived a little further away from school, in Gosnells, in the south-east of Perth. She was always available to me; I knew that if I rocked up at the teachers' lounge and she was there, I could just perch on the end of her desk and have a yarn, and she'd be OK with that.

So in the time between school finishing for the day and Follow the Dream starting, I hung around and pestered Jo at her desk, usually to tidy it up. She was such a messy person – her desk was always covered in stuff, which did my head in.

'How do you work like this?' I'd nag, and she'd laugh it off and let me tidy up her papers and stack them into neat piles.

I'd also get the afternoon snacks ready for Follow the Dream before everyone else arrived, boiling the kettle for Mi Goreng instant noodles, my favourite flavour, or pulling out the ingredients for nachos from the fridge, and stacking the food trolley with the fruit and other food the program provided for us.

The tutoring itself was really crucial for me, because my grades were suffering. Jo's initial goal for me was to improve my attendance and to catch up with the rest of my year. I wanted to learn and I was good at it, though I wasn't always fast, and I needed help getting into a routine and building the basic skills that I'd missed out on early in my schooling. I really credit Follow the Dream with pushing me when I really needed it, because over time, school gradually became easier and more manageable with the support of my tutors and Jo.

It was at Follow the Dream that Jo first encouraged me to run for the Student Representative Council for my year.

'You've gotta put your hand up for these things. No one else will do it for you,' she'd constantly remind me.

Her confidence in me gave me confidence in myself, so I nominated myself – and was then voted in by my peers. I felt so much pride when I first got elected, knowing that no one in my family had achieved anything like it. I wished I could tell Mum and Nan. They would have been so proud of their little girl.

The only times I ever missed Follow the Dream was when I was playing football. We had training a couple of times a week, and then games on the weekends. When I signed up for the footy program, I didn't realise how different it would be from back home. Bush football is a lot more casual than city football – in Carnarvon there were no uniforms, and often kids would play in bare feet if they didn't have boots. I remember running out onto the field in second-hand boots that were so big on me they were like flippers, and no one batted an eyelid.

The leap into a more organised team at school with formal drills and uniforms was a big change, but I loved the routine and the camaraderie that came with the team, something that would become more and more important in my life. Footy combined all the things I was good at – running and throwing, catching and kicking – and winning!

The only issue was that the girls team was small – a full team is eighteen players on the ground and there were only five of us, so the school coach, Jeremy Bruce, or 'Bruiser' as we called him, mixed us in with the boys team. Bruiser could see my potential as a player from the outset, as I had a natural ability and applied myself, and I was also a clear communicator on the field, calling for the ball and generally holding my own as a player with the boys. Bruiser would be a great support to me, encouraging me and helping me develop my game, and eventually I moved from ruck rover and wing positions to the forward line when I found my feet.

Football gave me so much confidence and structure. And just as I buried myself in athletics and netball at primary school, I threw myself into footy and the Student Representative Council as a way of moving forward and staying busy, which was often at odds with the activity that other young teenagers around me were occupied with – going out to parties, and the politics around friendships, not to mention the minefield of sex, which quite a few of my friends were getting up to at that age.

Year 8 turned into Year 9, and life at home was starting to feel a little strained with Leanne. Whenever she was angry with me or if we had an argument, she'd stop talking to me, and sometimes it could go on for days. To me, our arguments seemed to be over silly things; for instance, she'd make my lunch every day, but like most teenagers, half the time I wouldn't eat it. Either I'd be playing footy at lunchtime and forget, or a better offer would come along. Like most parents, she'd be cranky when she saw my lunch come back in my schoolbag. Why was she wasting time making me lunch if I wasn't going to eat it? Then she'd be silent and there'd be times when she wouldn't acknowledge me or reply when I spoke to her.

I'd agonise over what to do. I'd miss footy practice, I wouldn't see my friends. And then, suddenly, it would be over, and Leanne would be back to her usual loving self.

Looking back, I was used to dealing with conflict in a completely different way – when Mum was upset or angry with us, she simply flogged us, and that was that. I didn't know how to negotiate different responses when there was conflict, and whenever it happened, I'd get so anxious that I'd feel nauseous and I wouldn't be able to eat or sleep. I knew I was only living there by the grace of Leanne's considerable goodwill, and if she didn't want me there anymore, I worried about where I'd go next. Dad had left me with Leanne in the first place, so living with him wasn't an option, and I didn't want to leave the life I'd built in Armadale to move in with Grandma Susette, who was already looking after Troy. I couldn't ask her to take me on as well.

And Leanne was there for me in so many ways. She'd help me with my school assignments, whether it was buying the supplies I needed or helping me type up and print out essays out on the home printer. She helped me with skills I'd need as a young adult, too, helping me set up my first bank account, teaching me about how to use my card and the cheque book I got with it, which made me feel so grown up.

Around this time, I got my first real job. I knew I wanted to earn my own money, to start taking care of myself and reduce the burden on Leanne, but I had no idea how to go about it. Talking to Jo one afternoon in one of our Follow the Dream sessions, she filled me in.

'Well, the first thing you need is a resume,' she told me.

Like most teens, I had no clue what that was, so Jo helped me to write one up, listing all my skills and my achievements from school, including the delivery run with Sam. Then we printed out copies, and I handed them out at as many outlets as I could at the local shopping centre in Armadale.

When I approached the front desk at Target, I was lucky enough to chat to the manager, a friendly woman called

Winona – we clicked, and the next day I got a call from her, and a job offer. So between school, my Student Representative Council duties, footy and work, I had an even busier schedule, and I was also able to start giving Leanne some board, about $20 out of every pay cheque.

Over this time, I was in and out of touch with my siblings. I didn't hear much from Eden, who was now living and working up Karratha way, and RJ was still so young and living with his dad in Carnarvon, so there wasn't much opportunity to connect with him. But Troy was living with Grandma Susette in Perth, and I'd call and talk to him whenever I could. Because Susette lived all the way over on the other side of Perth, it was hard for me to get over to see him but once I was working I could afford to pay the bus fare, and would sometimes trek out on the weekend to watch him play football. By the time I got my first mobile phone, he had my number and could get in touch, too.

One day when I was in class, my phone rang – it was Troy. I sneaked out to take the call.

'Sis, I'm in Armadale,' Troy told me. He was calling from the payphone at the train station.

'What the hell are you doing here?' I hissed back. 'Why aren't you in school?'

Then it became clear – he'd had an argument with Grandma Susette that morning, and had run away from home.

For the first time ever, I crept out of school so I could go and get him. Troy was stoked to see me, though he still copped an earful about running away. I took him back to Leanne's and gave him a feed while we rang Susette and waited for her to come and pick him up (and gave him another earful about stressing poor Grandma Susette out). It felt so good being his big sister again, but I felt terrible for skipping school.

Ky also popped up around this time. As far as I knew then, Ky was either homeless or crashing with mates here and there, but somehow she'd found our address and one afternoon, when I got home from school, there she was. It happened to be on one of the rare occasions when Dad was there, too.

She smiled her cheeky smile at me, and wrapped me in a hug. 'Just wanted to see you, sis,' she said softly.

I was so shocked. I hadn't seen Ky in such a long time. But what jolted me most was how much she looked like Mum, and it was gut wrenching to see her. It turned out she'd been in and out of Graylands Hospital, a dedicated mental health service in Perth, and she was a bit spacey and out of it, which was either the drugs, or her disintegrating mental health; her schizophrenia would have been getting worse by then. I have a photograph from her visit that day, which I treasure – it's one of the only images I have of me and my big sister together, the two of us in Leanne's kitchen.

After dinner with the entire family – Dad, Leanne, Tye, Kallom and me – Ky left that night, as suddenly as she'd arrived, and I didn't see her again for a while.

These interludes with my siblings, or the brief moments I'd see or hear from someone in Carnarvon, would throw me out of my routine. I was working so hard to keep everything at bay – my grief and what I know now was post-traumatic stress from the assault – that any little trigger could spark me spiralling. But I'd figured out by then that if I just kept on going on the hamster wheel of school-sport-work-friends and never gave myself time to think, I could push all the hard feelings to one side.

And of course, as I was getting older, other things were starting to occupy my mind, like romance and relationships. I wasn't dating anyone, though I'd had feelings by then for a few people, including some girls, which I didn't think about too deeply. Like most fifteen-year-olds, I was still figuring myself out, and it wasn't the easiest time to confront the idea that I could be bisexual or be sexually interested in girls.

Then, at the end of that year, I fell head over heels for a boy. His name was Dom.

We met at a state football competition. By now, I'd starting playing club football for South Fremantle, for their girls Under 16s team. I loved playing football for the school team, and I got along well with the everyone, girls and guys alike. We all trained together and were friends, but the boys could be such show ponies when they were playing! They'd fool around and talk rubbish, which could be quite intimidating for the other girls, though not for me. I just wanted to play, and play well.

Our coach, Bruiser, encouraged me to be more of a mentor for the other girls. By then I was in Year 10 and still making headway on the student representative council. He'd say to me, 'You're Year 10 captain, right? So be a leader on the field too!'

I loved motivating the girls on the team, and our game improved so much that Bruiser encouraged us to sign up to a proper club, outside of the school competition. Club footy at South Fremantle was another step up. I thrived learning new skills and techniques, proper tackles and plays, and embraced the discipline and commitment to the team. I absolutely loved the intensity of what club footy asked of me, and my first game in the competition is such a strong memory for me. It was on a weekend not long after I joined the team, and Dad actually came to watch me, which I was pretty psyched about. But as I'd discover, it would be the first and the last time he ever saw me play.

Not long after I joined South Fremantle, I got the chance to try out for the Western Australia Under 16s State team. When I started in the team at school, I never dreamed that I could be good enough to play footy at such an advanced level, and it *was* like a dream when I aced the tryouts and found out that I'd made the team! I was so thrilled – if only I could've told Nan – but making the team came hand in hand with a problem. In order to participate, I'd need to buy the full kit – and it cost $500, which was a fortune to me, and to Leanne.

'Well, we'll just have to figure it out,' Leanne said when I told her. We put our heads together, and we came up with a plan.

Leanne helped me apply for a school grant, which I won, and that covered half of the cost. I pulled together what I'd saved from work at Target, and she put in the rest. And when the full kit arrived, it felt like Christmas to me. As I pulled out each item – jersey, socks and shorts – I was in awe. I wanted to wear that jersey everywhere, and I probably would have if Leanne hadn't talked some sense into me!

That year the State Championships were held in Perth at Lathlain Park, the home of the Perth Demons (and later, the West Coast Eagles), which was lucky for me. If the competition had been held anywhere else in the country, I don't think our plan would have covered the travel and accommodation costs of travelling interstate to compete.

The comp was played over a weekend; two days of round-robin games, culminating in the final, and I was so stoked to be part of such a talented team of girls, representing my state in the game I loved, and it was extra special for me personally as a big first for my family. We got knocked out of the comp pretty quickly, and Vic Metro, the team representing Victoria, went on to win the championship.

It was on the first day of the comp that I met Dom, though paradoxically I was actually beginning to question my sexuality. Joining the state team, I'd met another player, BJ, who stirred the first strong feelings I'd ever had for a girl. The first time I met BJ, I felt an instant attraction to her – she was such a cheeky character, funny and sarcastic, and we became fast friends. BJ wasn't like the rest of the girls on our team, and neither was I – we were both a little rough around the edges and had come from the same kind of background. I think we clicked knowing that we had that in common, and we were as thick as thieves. I even let her cut my hair into a choppy mullet just like hers (which Leanne didn't love!).

As we sat in the crowd between our games at the State Championships, BJ and I were shooting the breeze and bantering as we always did, joking about the plays and players on the field. I didn't realise anyone could hear us until I heard a chuckle behind us, and I turned around to see two guys, around our age, who were smirking at what we were saying.

One of them was cute, with short brown hair and a cheeky face.

He caught my eye and grinned. 'Not pulling any punches, are you?' he teased.

I couldn't help smirking back, and that was that, until a week later at training at school when Richard, one of the guys who played on the State team, told me that Dom, the cheeky guy with the brown hair, had been asking about me.

'He's jerpin' for you,' Richard teased, using a slang word for 'crushing'. Richard was First Nations like me, and we were mates. We called him Black Magic because he was such a speedy bugger on the field.

And not long after, when I was on MSN messenger chatting with my friends, I got a ping from Dom.

'Hey, how are you?'

'Hey, State hotshot,' I replied. I was always sassy!

It all happened pretty quickly, and I was absolutely giddy with my first romance. We were together as much as we could be – Dom's parents were separated, so he lived in Kalgoorlie with his dad and went to school there, and he'd visit his mum and play footy in Perth – and if we couldn't see each other, we'd stay up late chatting on the house phone, or write each other long messages on MSN (back then text messages cost an absolute mint). I've still got the letters we sent to each other in the first flush of love.

Sometimes I wonder whether I threw myself into a relationship with Dom as a way of pushing aside the feelings I had for BJ. But even though I loved the way I felt around her, there was no way I would have considered the idea of us dating. No one close to me was gay, and the kids at school who were had to deal with homophobic jokes and comments; even teachers weren't immune from making the occasional homophobic comment. I was so young, and I didn't have the resources or positive influences to help me, so I often wonder whether the choice I made about my sexuality then was a result of the expectation around me. But I genuinely liked boys, especially Dom.

I don't think there's anything quite like your first love, especially as a teenager. When I met Dom, I fell in love hard, to the point of obsession. But importantly, I felt accepted; like I'd found 'my' person. For someone who had been dealt so much trauma so early in my life, I can't overstate how much this meant to me. My heart needed someone to latch on to, and Dom gave me the crucial, unconditional sense of love and security that I needed, something that had been missing in my life ever since Nan had died. Perhaps more than that, the love he gave me was something I'd never had before – something private and special, something that existed only between the two of us. No one could take that away from me, or ruin what I felt.

Before I met Dom, I didn't know what a respectful romantic relationship looked like. Sure, I'd seen idealised love in movies, but even then I knew it didn't reflect reality, and a lot of the 'love' I'd witnessed around me growing up was toxic. Mum's relationships were chaotic to say the least; and so were Nan's. With Leanne and Dad separated, they weren't going to win couple of the year either, so the role models I had weren't up to the job of showing me what a generous and kind relationship could be.

But remarkably, with Dom, that's exactly what we had, and we wanted to spend all our time together when we could. I even travelled out to Kalgoorlie to visit him and meet his family there. I told Dom more about my life and my past than I had with anyone, and while I knew he was shocked, he never once judged me, even though his life was so much more 'normal' than mine. I can still remember the heady rush of receiving a message from him, and not being able to hide my smile. I'd never considered myself sentimental, but when I was with Dom, I loved the moments we spent gooey-eyed, talking about an imagined future together – getting married, having kids. It's funny to look back at those fantasies now, because we were literally children, but God, did it feel real then!

But falling in love with Dom also meant that I started losing focus at school. My attendance started to get patchy again, and I wasn't putting the effort in that I usually did – and in the end, it created problems at home with Leanne.

We were already getting into arguments fairly often by then. The older I was getting, the more I was asserting myself and starting to push back against the rules at home. Inevitably we'd end up arguing, Leanne would stop talking to me and I'd rocket from feeling stronger and more confident to feeling like the scared little girl who was begging to be saved from Mum's wake. Now I was spending so much time with Dom, Leanne and I clashed over how long I was on the computer and phone, and obsessing over him.

And then, one night, we had an argument which escalated to the point of no return. I can't remember what it was about, but it was a doozy. Being the teen I was, all I wanted was to make decisions for myself, something I'd always had to do growing up in Carnarvon, and at the time I felt suffocated, a mess of anger and stress. I couldn't bear to be there for one second longer, which in the end would be to my detriment and something I would have to work out on my own in the coming weeks.

I grabbed a black garbage bag and went to my room, and started throwing stuff in there – clothes, my uniform, my school books, my footy gear. With a pang of regret I looked at my beautiful dresser, neatly set with bottles of cream and perfume, but it didn't last long. Soon Leanne and I were shouting at each other again, and I stormed out of the house.

'Go and live with your dad then!' she called after me.

'I will!'

Even as I was stomping away, trying to call Dad, dread was forming a heavy weight in my stomach. Dad was living in a caravan park in Kelmscott, an hour away on foot, and I'd only been there once or twice. I had no idea how he was going to react to me showing up.

I ended up catching a bus and walking the rest of the way, jittery with nerves. It was getting dark, and I felt cold, anxiety making me shiver. Finally I arrived – it was an average Aussie caravan park, pretty run down and dodgy, but a haven for people who needed a roof over their heads and had no hope of affording a regular place to rent on their own.

There was a block of shared toilets and showers, and then rows of caravans and cabins. Dad's caravan was the same as all the rest, and he was waiting for me when I got there. Leanne would have called him as soon as I'd left.

'What have you done this time?'

'Can I stay here?' I asked, avoiding his eye. I didn't want him to see how much I needed him to say yes.

He sighed. 'Yeah. All right.'

Inside, there was a small 'living' area and the kitchenette, and two sleeping areas at each end of the van. I took the front half and Dad took the back, and as I crawled onto the mattress and under the cover, I curled myself up to be as small as possible. I was used to that. I was grateful for my phone at least, and could text Dom in Kalgoorlie. I didn't tell him what had happened. I didn't want him to know just how wrecked my life was, but texting him made me feel less alone.

The next few weeks were hard. Though he wasn't home a lot, I'd never lived with Dad on my own for any length of time. I'm sure he and Leanne discussed what to do about me, and he tried a few times to exert a level of parental control, but he'd never been much of a parent to me, so that wasn't going to fly.

I stayed out for as long as I could, at school, at footy training. I was still working at Target, working on Thursday nights until 9 pm, and I'd have to get the bus back home late at night. It was pretty dodgy in that part of town and I'd walk the kilometre or so from the bus stop to Dad's caravan on my own.

The caravan park didn't feel particularly safe either, especially when I was on my own – the lock on the caravan door was pretty flimsy, and anyone could break in if they were desperate enough, so I felt anxious most of the time. Whenever I went to the shower blocks I'd take my phone with me so I could play music – my favourite song at the time, 'Airplanes' by B.o.B. – to help me feel less alone and creeped out in the quiet darkness of the shower cubicle.

Life wasn't particularly great for Dad; he wasn't in a good place either. He'd quit yet another job, and he was drinking a lot.

The final straw came when I got home from school one day and found the door to the caravan ajar. I kept what little cash I had in a tin with my things, and that afternoon I found it on the floor of the van, open – and empty.

That money, hard-earned from my work at Target, was one of the few things I could control, the only thing of value I owned. The independence it gave me was crucial – at the very least, I needed it to pay for the bus to get to footy training and work, and when I saw it gone, I felt so bleak. My stomach felt like a black pit, and I wanted to weep, but I knew there was no point. I needed to act.

Instead I got the bin bag out again, and started throwing my things in it, my mind buzzing with stress. Where would I go? I couldn't go back to Leanne's.

One of my best friends was a guy called Corey, and he was probably the only other person who knew what my full story was, other than Dom. Corey was a funny kid, a little quirky, and from the moment we met in our first year of school, we clicked. We'd often chat on MSN, and when I wasn't at footy training or at Follow the Dream, I'd go to his house after school where his mum and dad were so kind and welcoming – they even gave me a Christmas present every year.

That night, weighing up my options in the caravan, I decided to call Corey. It made me cringe with embarrassment to have to admit that I needed help, but I had no other options, and I knew he wouldn't judge me.

To my relief, he didn't hesitate. 'Come over to mine,' he said immediately. 'You can stay with us. Mum won't mind.'

Before I left, I took one last glance around the caravan. All I had to my name could be carried in the garbage bag in my hand. I didn't know what Dad would say, and I had no idea what my next move would be, but I knew the only person I could rely on was me.

So that's what I did. It wasn't my first step into the unknown, but it was the first one I took as a young adult, making a choice for myself.

Five

Another house, another bed. When I found myself homeless, living out of a bin bag and crashing in Corey's spare room, I wondered whether it had always been coming. Life had been going too well for me. Things had been so settled; I'd been living such a normal experience as a teenager. But my life had never been easy, and it was as if I'd been waiting for something to go wrong.

So when everything went up in flames, I just went with it. Dad didn't try to get me to move back in with him, and I wasn't speaking to Leanne. So it was easy, then, to stop going to school, and to start missing my Follow the Dream sessions with Jo. I kept going to footy training and to work, but for a few weeks I didn't do much else. There were parties to go to every so often, and I was seeing Dom whenever he was in Perth.

It felt as if I'd only been holding on by a thread for the last few years, the routine of living with Leanne the only anchor that was keeping me from floating away. And now, with that thread snapped, I just couldn't figure out what the point of it all was. Sure, I could go to school, and try and keep up with my studies, but I didn't have anywhere long-term to live. I was only able to stay at Corey's place thanks to the goodwill of his mum, and that would eventually run out because it wasn't fair to expect her to take me on, a virtual stranger.

If I turned up at Grandma Susette's, would she have space for another child? She was already looking after Troy. And if I went back to Carnarvon, to live with Dragan, or Aunty Ricki or Aunty Katrina, what would happen then? How long would it be before I dropped out of school anyway, or fell pregnant? How was I meant to break the cycle if I was back in exactly the same place, the same circumstances, as Mum, or as Ky?

I didn't want to leave Perth, and I definitely didn't want to leave my school. I finally had friends, a community of people. I loved playing footy, and I loved having a job and earning my own money. But no matter how long I puzzled over it, I couldn't see a way out of the situation I was in. I wouldn't be able to find somewhere to live on my own. I was only sixteen. Technically, I should have been put into the child welfare system, but the thought of another foster home made my heart race with anxiety.

So I did what lots of young people do in a crisis. I shut down. I loafed around at Corey's when he went to school, and prayed for some sort of a miracle.

It was only a few weeks before Jo tracked me down. I'd prayed for a miracle, and I got one, even though I didn't recognise it at the time.

Jo had been tracking my absences at Follow the Dream, and was keeping an eye out for me. But when I failed to turn up for school by the second week, she decided enough was enough, and that Friday she found Corey at school. He told her where I was, and the next thing she was at the front door of his house, calling my name.

'What's all this, then?' she asked, in her usual brisk way, when I came out. 'Why are you missing school?'

I shrugged, sullen, trying to tough it out. It was embarrassing standing outside a house that wasn't even mine, with my teacher. Then I felt as if I'd cry if Jo pushed me too hard, and I think she sensed that, too, because her voice softened.

'Look, I've signed you up for Outward Bound, and it's on next week. I want you to go.'

I'd completely forgotten about it. Outward Bound was a leadership program for high school students and was focused on outdoor education – week-long hikes, camping and navigating in the wilderness where you learn skills like bushcraft and survival strategies, and about connecting to country. Jo had been pushing me to sign up for it for ages.

'It'll be good for you, Brooke,' she continued. 'It'll get you out of your head, teach you some life skills. And it counts towards your WACE, don't forget that bit.' The WACE, the Western Australian Certificate of Education, is the equivalent of the Higher School Certificate, the HSC, in the eastern states.

Even though I'd been trying to do my best at school, I'd been very distracted since I'd met Dom and I was only just scraping by with my schoolwork. It would be a big push to get a decent university entrance score, so I could use the extra points wherever I could find them.

'I don't have any of the camping gear, or walking boots,' I reminded her.

'That doesn't matter, Brooke, we can sort that out,' Jo said firmly. 'I'll pick you up on Monday.' Then she caught my eye. 'It *will* be good for you,' she repeated.

I sighed, and then nodded slowly. I could never say no to Jo – and I knew something needed to change. For the last couple of weeks, I'd been struggling to make decisions for myself. Realistically I was too young to be out on my own, and I was frozen, in stasis, which seemed the safest thing to do. If I didn't do anything, then nothing could go wrong.

Jo was right. Outward Bound *was* good for me; it shook me out of that way of thinking completely. A couple of days later, true to her word, Jo rocked up in her Honda Captiva, with a back seat full of camping gear that she'd bought or borrowed for me.

'Ready?' she asked, from the driver's seat.

I said my goodbyes to Corey, and climbed into the passenger seat, caught between reluctance and relief that something was happening to yank me out of my slump.

'What's all this?' I asked, nodding towards the back seat.

'Got you a sleeping bag, some hiking shoes, and some other gear for when you're out in the bush,' Jo said, turning the car onto the road.

I sniffed, scrunching my nose. 'What's the smell?' It wasn't exactly unpleasant, but it was a musty, animal sort of smell.

'That'll be the horses,' Jo replied, shrugging. 'Car's usually full of hay and feed and their blankets.'

I remembered Jo's passion for horses. Now I could definitely smell the earthy, farm scent.

'Your car is as bad as your desk,' I muttered, and Jo grinned.

'There's the Brooke I know,' she said, and for a minute my throat felt tight.

Soon we pulled up a local bus stop where there was a coach waiting for the Outward Bound participants. There were only two other kids there, a boy and a girl who were my age, so it was going to be a very small group, and I wasn't sure if that made me feel better about it or worse. On one hand, it was fewer people to deal with. But on the other, there'd be nowhere to hide. I'd really have to participate.

Jo kept the car running for a second, and I paused before I got out, suddenly feeling inert all over again.

'Hey, listen,' Jo said, turning her body to face me better. 'You go out there and try and learn something about yourself. I think you'll be surprised.'

'Yeah, OK,' I said. I tried to look more enthusiastic. 'I'll do my best.'

'And when you get back, we'll sort everything else out,' Jo said decisively.

I looked at her, confused. 'What do you mean?'

'I'll pick you up when you get back, and we'll go from there,' Jo said. 'Now, off you go. And have fun.'

I grabbed my stuff from the back of the car, and waved at Jo, turning her words over in my mind. For the first time in weeks, I felt something lightening in my chest. The dread I was carrying was easing a tiny bit. If Jo was going to help me sort things out, I wasn't alone in the mess I'd found myself in. I didn't know what was next, but at least I had someone in my corner.

Now, I'd like to say that Outward Bound was one hundred per cent enjoyable, but I'd be lying! Roughing it in the bush was challenging. While I like a bit of camping, I'm probably more of a campsite-with-a-proper-toilet kind of girl. But if I put my creature comforts to one side, those five days in the bush were another turning point for me. In a lot of ways, they changed my life.

The guides taught us about navigation and surviving out in the bush, but we also talked a lot about mindset and planning, our futures and goals.

We were hiking a small part of the Bibbulmun Track, which stretches all the way from Kalamunda on the outskirts of Perth to Albany on the southern tip of Western Australia, and the landscape was breathtaking. There were parts where we'd just be walking through bush on trails, often single file and focussing on the burn of our legs and the feeling of breath in our lungs as we pushed through to our physical limits. Then, after getting ourselves to the top of a hill, a beautiful, sprawling view would open up. I remember one vista in particular at the top of a hill at Walpole, where we saw the entire landscape spread out all around us – the beautiful bush of Noongar country stretching out to one side, and mountains on the other, rolling down to give way to the coast, simply nature as far as the eye could see.

There was something so restorative about that view. Standing in the open air, the breeze touching my skin and the sunlight gentle and golden around us, I felt such a strong sense of country, of being connected to the earth under my feet and every living creature on it. I suddenly knew there was strength in me that would never go away. There was so much to fight for, to push for in life. All this time I had been feeling as if I was at a crossroads, paralysed and waiting to be swept along one path or another, but now, for the first time, I could see it was in my power to *choose* the direction I would travel in.

Would I choose to take the hard path – to persevere with school, to act with discipline and focus to carve out a better life for myself? Or would I refuse to make a choice at all, and just let life happen to me? Go to the parties, drink, experiment, allow my youth to be wasted and my future limited?

Standing there, I was reminded of the goals I'd set myself when I'd first started high school. Everything I had achieved so far, at school, with footy, had all been for my family. I wanted to be a role model for Troy and RJ, and I wanted to show them that our family could do more, *be* more, than what we'd seen around us growing up. I wanted to show them that education meant something, and that there were so many more options than drugs and alcohol to guide our lives.

More than that, I wanted to make something of myself for Mum and for Nan. They were both products of their environments, and they'd each lost so much as a result of their battles with addiction, with violent relationships, and with poverty. But I could choose a different life. I could use this opportunity to gain my education, and lift myself out of directionlessness and poverty. I could do it for them, and for my brothers – but most importantly I could do it for *me*. I knew there was more out there for me, and standing on that hill at the tender age of sixteen I knew I was at crucial fork in the road. Either I committed to choosing a strong path for myself, or I gave up and let it all go.

Later that night, sitting around the campfire and grazing on trailmix, I listened to the other students as they talked about their worries. The other kids were concerned about things like disappointing their parents, not being smart enough to get the grades they wanted, about choosing a career path after school – normal teenage anxieties. I was worried about where I'd live – how I'd live – when I got back to Perth. Jo had said she'd help me sort everything out when I got back, but I didn't really know what that meant. Would I be back in Corey's spare room until his mum's patience ran out? Or would I have to go begging back to Leanne's? That didn't feel like an option at all. I'm sure we could have worked out our differences, but I also knew I needed a change.

I watched the fire flicker away, and let the sounds of everyone talking turn into grey noise. I lifted my head to take in the inky night sky above us, glittering with stars, and that same feeling of calm from earlier in the day washed over me again.

I truly believe that country can heal, and sitting there, with a fire in front of me and the night sky stretching overhead, I felt more strength restored to me. I was ready to go back and work out the mess of my life.

On the bus ride home, I tried not to worry about what was next. I just needed to focus on one thing at a time, and make the best choices I could.

True to Jo's word, when we pulled into the bus top, there was her Honda Captiva, small and rusty and probably full of horse feed ... And there was Jo, leaning against the bonnet, waiting for me.

'So, was it life changing, or what?' she greeted me, giving me a one-armed hug in her gruff way.

'It was pretty good,' I mumbled. I was so relieved to see her, I didn't know what else to say.

'I spoke to Leanne and Bruiser,' she said, answering my unasked question. 'We think it's best you come to live with me for a bit.'

I nodded, trying not to overreact. 'Thanks,' I said. 'That sounds good.'

I can't describe the sheer relief I felt getting into Jo's car. All the anxiety of the last few weeks started ebbing away, and I think I realised for the first time just how much stress I'd been holding inside me.

'Now, I have rules,' Jo said, as we drove out of the carpark. 'The first one is, you have to go to school. No excuses, and no wagging. You're going to graduate Year 12.'

I nodded. I wanted to – but I knew I couldn't motivate myself to do it without someone pushing me, especially when I was feeling as low as I had been.

'The second rule is, if you're going out to see anyone, or go partying, or whatever, I need to know where you are, and when you'll be home. And the third rule is, you have to help me with the horses, otherwise we'll be running late every morning and eating at midnight every night!'

I grinned. I could see that life with Jo was going to be a bit different to what I was used to with Leanne, but truth be told, I needed that structure and order now. And how bad could the horses be?

Jo lived in Gosnells, about twenty minutes further down the highway from Armadale. Her house was small and cosy, and there was a spare room set up that had previously housed another student, Bridget, who Jo had been guardian of a year or so earlier. I wasn't the only one lucky enough to have her looking out for me. Clearly she had a history of picking up strays and helping them get their lives in order.

Maybe that was why she didn't have kids of her own, I wondered, because she was meant to be there for kids like me.

I walked behind Jo through the house, clutching my bag of gear, while she pointed out the amenities.

'There's a bed, and a set of drawers, and a desk in there,' she said at the door of what would be my room. 'You can make it your own if you like, I don't mind you decorating it a bit. And if there's something you need, you just need to tell me, and we'll see what we can do.'

I went in, and dumped my bag on the floor, and took the room in.

Another new room. Another new start. I decided there and then that I wasn't going to take this second chance for granted. I would choose the path that was laid out in front of me. I wanted to find whatever it was that Jo saw in me. I was going to make her, and Mum and Nan – and myself – proud.

Jo applied formally to be my guardian. The principal of my high school, Richard Hunter, agreed with her that it was the best course of action for me, and they spoke to Leanne and Dad, who signed the relevant paperwork.

I was so glad and relieved to have a home with Jo, and I'm sure Leanne and Dad did what they felt was the best thing for me.

And it turned out it *was* the best thing for me. Living with Jo was a balm, and just what I needed – life was calm and structured, and best of all she didn't try to parent me; she saw me for who I was. She didn't sweat the small stuff and gave me the autonomy I craved, but she was also clear about her expectations about pulling my weight around the house and getting my schoolwork done. I had so much respect for Jo – I really looked up to her, not only as an inspiring teacher and mentor, but also as someone with goals and ambitions of her own.

As her house was small, we shared a bathroom, and sometimes that felt a little awkward, but Jo was so matter-of-fact it swiftly became normal. I made my bedroom feel a bit more like my own straight away, sticking photos and posters up on the walls – snapshots of happy times with my family and friends, and posters of my favourite bands, like Blink 182 and Good Charlotte (I was in my punky, EMO phase, after all) and kick-arse female performers like Beyonce, Christina Aguilera, and most beloved of all, Alicia Keyes. And I enjoyed the fact that there was no ugly pink wallpaper!

Days started early with Jo because we had to feed her horses before driving in to school. She had three horses; one lived further away on a property in the Lesmurdie hills, which didn't need much taking care of, and the other two, Buddy and Ray, were agisted at a property nearby in Gosnells.

Jo would get me up before dawn, and I'd be bleary-eyed in the car, rugged up over my uniform against the chilly morning air. She had such a strong nurturing instinct, and she had a real knack for animals – she was soft and gentle with her horses, and I could see why they loved and trusted her. I got comfortable around the big animals pretty quickly; helping out with the chores was non-negotiable and part of our agreement when I came to live with her.

When we arrived, we'd take off their rugs and muck out their stalls in the stable, and then feed them – a complicated concoction of molasses and hay and other mysterious supplements. I loved the challenge of remembering the sequence and measurements of the ingredients, a meditative task that Jo patiently taught me, which I was doing on my own in no time. Then we'd walk them out into the paddock for the day, where they'd stay until the afternoon, when we'd come back after school to return them to the stable for the night.

It wasn't the first time I'd spent any time with horses – in Carnarvon, being a country town, there were a few families who had horses or lived on properties with animals. There was one very memorable experience in particular that I'd had with a pony, which I told Jo about early one morning.

One afternoon after school, when I was eight or nine, I was hanging out with some other kids at the little playground in town, when a girl I was friends with, Harriet, arrived with her mum and her pony, a cute little grey thing. Harriet was so proud to be showing her pony off and, being the adventurous kid I was, I immediately asked if I could have a ride. These days parents are probably a bit more cautious, but Harriet's mum said, 'Sure, hop on!' There was no saddle, and I didn't have a helmet, but that wasn't going to stop me, so I climbed up on the balance beam in the playground for height and threw a leg over the pony.

Off we went, walking around, but I must have accidentally kicked my little steed, because in a split second it had taken off and I was clinging on to its mane for dear life. Being a clever pony, he made straight for the grown-ups – no doubt thinking, 'Get this kid off me!' – and then flew straight over the balance beam. I have no idea how I didn't fall off and break a bone.

When I'd proudly finished telling Jo that story, she gave me a sceptical look. 'Hmm. Maybe we won't get you riding them just yet.'

I did get to ride the horses eventually. Jo had problems with her back and her neck, which meant she couldn't ride anymore, but once she knew the horses trusted me, she got me out in the paddock on Buddy, first leading me around the yard and then showing me how to raise him to a trot, and finally a canter. She was such a naturally gifted teacher, and she loved those horses so much, she was in her element teaching me how to look after them and to ride. Jo bought me my first pair of jodhpurs, which I barely took off for a while.

In the evenings, after putting the horses back to stable, we'd head home and cook dinner together, usually comfort food like pasta, and the traditional Aussie dinner, meat and three veg, and chat about our day as we ate. Then we'd move to the couch and enjoy some trashy TV.

'You can sit with me,' Jo told me, 'but you have to get your homework done too.' So I'd bring my books out to the lounge and do my work with the comforting sound of the television in the background.

At school, I reapplied myself and tried to make up for lost time. By then I was in Year 11, and the next two years were going to the hardest academically, so Follow the Dream became my haven, where I could make my way through what felt like a mountain of schoolwork with the help of my tutors – and Jo, of course. With her encouragement, I also applied for traineeship in administration, which would count as credit towards my WACE. It was a good way of keeping my options open, even while I was studying to get a university entrance score.

Once afternoon a week, I worked at an antenatal clinic at Armadale Hospital doing admin work. It was dry stuff, data entry and scanning patient medical records. But I learned the work quickly and I was efficient, and I enjoyed the methodical routine of it. It reminded me of all those hours spent folding catalogues with Sam in our delivery-girl days. I was still working nights and weekends at Target, which meant I had some spare cash too, most of which I was trying to save, and Jo always made time to pick me up after my shifts.

'Was your dad picking you up when you worked late?' she asked me once, not long after I first moved in with her.

'Nah,' I said. 'I was catching the bus, and then walking the rest of the way to the caravan park.'

Jo stared at me. 'At night? By yourself?'

Her expression said it all, and from then on, she was always there at the end of my shifts to pick me up, even though it was a good half-hour drive out of her way. I knew then that Jo would always be there for me – she didn't take my guardianship lightly, and adjusted her own life to be available when I needed her. I'm so grateful for the care she gave me.

Meanwhile, I was still playing AFL for South Fremantle, and I was still gunning for Head Girl, though considering my previous year, I was pretty convinced I'd missed the boat.

But Jo had faith. 'OK, so you made a few mistakes. That's human,' she reminded me. 'It's what you do now that counts. So get going on that application!'

You had to nominate yourself for Head Girl, then write a pitch about why you were the best candidate, and take part in an interview with the principal, head teachers and the president of the P&C. I was a little reluctant, because I couldn't see how I was going to win it after missing so much school when I was homeless, and generally dropping the ball.

But whenever I voiced my doubts, Jo would say, 'Brooke, you can't give up on your goals so easily.'

She reminded me that I had set this particular target all the way back in my first year of high school, and that I had worked hard to do my bit for the school on the Student Representative Council ever since then.

'Just because you've had setbacks doesn't mean you shouldn't still try.'

It was hard to argue with her when she was making so much sense! So I plucked up my courage, put my application in, and did the interview – and I surprised myself. Once I started answering the questions from the panel in the interview, I realised that I'd achieved and contributed a lot over the last four years – I'd been a vocal representative of the student body with the P&C and the school board, had contributed pieces for the school's monthly newsletter, and often addressed the entire school at assembly to hand out awards and merit certificates. I'd won merit certificates myself for leadership, had attended science and engineering camps at the University of Western Australia, and just the year before I'd travelled to Canberra for work experience, working with Rachel Siewert, a Western Australian senator for the Greens.

Despite all this, I was shocked when, not long after, I was announced as Head Girl at assembly. Hearing my name read out was surreal, as was standing up in front of all my peers and walking up to the stage to receive my pin.

My friends and fellow students clapped and cheered for me, and standing there on the stage, I felt at once feeling awkward at the all the attention and overwhelmed with pride at my achievement. As I shook hands with Principal Hunter and accepted my pin, I could barely wipe the grin off my face, but as I turned to look at the audience, filled with the cheering family members of other students winning awards that day, my stomach dropped.

Mum was gone, and so was Nan. Dad and Leanne didn't know what I was up to; I hadn't seen or spoken to them since I'd left

Leanne's months ago. My brothers and sister were all scattered across the state. For a moment, I faltered. I felt so alone, and it's always hard to celebrate when you're on your own.

But then I caught sight of Jo, from where she sat with the other teachers at the side of the auditorium with the other teachers. She was clapping hard for me, and her face was shining with pride. My heart ballooned. It meant so much that she was there for me, and I shook off my sadness and owned the moment, standing proudly next to the newly elected Head Boy, Mitchell Davies, for our photos to be taken.

Being made Head Girl marked another turning point for me, this time with school. It filled me with so much pride to see my name engraved on the plaque in the teachers' lounge – a potent symbol of everything I had overcome to get to that point. With the pride of my achievement buoying me, I got back into a strong rhythm and applied myself to my schoolwork with a new fervour. Studying still didn't come very easily to me, but I always made sure I attended Follow the Dream and did my homework. And it all started paying off – my marks improved and I started catching up to my peers. Soon I was getting letters of commendation for my improvement in academic performance, and to top it all off I made it into the state footy team again, this time for the Under 18s.

Meanwhile, I was still dating Dom, and our relationship was starting to get more serious. We'd been together for over a year now, and Dom was ready for us to go to the next level. While I'd made a pact with myself to wait before having sex, I was over sixteen now, but something was still holding me back. Like any teenagers, things would get hot and heavy between us, but I found myself putting on the brakes before anything really happened.

'It's cool, no pressure,' Dom would say, but I still *felt* pressure. He was trying his best to be respectful, but I loved him, and I hated disappointing him. And I did want to have sex. But I also didn't want to get pregnant, and for everything I'd worked so hard for to go up in a puff of smoke.

Then another complicating factor arrived, in the form of Teneille.

We met at footy. I'd been playing for South Fremantle for a couple of years by now, and over that time the team had changed, with players leaving and new girls joining. I was an established member of the team, one of the longer serving members.

One day, there was a new girl at practice. She was a similar size to me, petite, and she was culturally diverse too. From the moment I saw her, I was floored. Something about this girl triggered a reaction in me – I immediately wanted to know her, and be around her.

'Hey,' she said casually, nodding at me while we stretched before starting practice. 'I'm Teneille.'

'Brooke,' I said, smiling back. And I swear, from that moment, we were inseparable.

Teneille wasn't like any girl I'd been friends with before. She was outgoing and fun, but she was also a really loving person, too, affectionate and sweet. And she thought I was the bee's knees – from the get-go, she told me she thought I was beautiful, that she admired me, and I felt the same way about her. *Everything* about Teneille was amazing to me.

She and I would hang out at practice, and then back at Jo's place. Sometimes we'd go to her house too, which was very different to Jo's. Tenielle's family was clearly wealthy, and she had everything a teenage girl could dream of – a huge, well-appointed house, with a pool in the front yard, and she even had her own car, a little black Suzuki Swift. I remember that car clearly, because it seemed she had so little regard for it. She'd spill coffee in it and just let it sink into the carpet – even now if I smell off milk, I think of Tenielle's Suzuki Swift!

Teneille was a bit of a tomboy, and really athletic. As well as playing football, she also did martial arts and she had an impressive six-pack from all the exercise she did. But underneath her tough exterior, she was a total softie. We'd spend hours talking, but equally we were just as comfortable in silence, quiet with our own thoughts. I'd never felt that ease before, not even with Dom, despite our long-term relationship. I felt I could be utterly myself when I was with Teneille.

Soon, though, our relationship was crossing into unfamiliar territory. I couldn't deny I was attracted to her, and as much as I tried to push that aside, it was hard to ignore when we were spending so much time cuddling on the couch. It could easily have been dismissed as just two teenage girls developing a close friendship, but to me it was more than just friendly affection – it was bordering on the romantic. I thought Teneille was beautiful, and I wanted to be with her constantly, but these feelings confused me and stressed me out – I was with Dom, who I loved, and who loved me.

Teneille's arrival in my life sparked the first time I really questioned my sexuality. The feelings I'd had for girls until then had been easy to ignore or justify as just being part of a 'girl crush', admiration that wasn't sexual or romantic. Bisexuality wasn't something I'd ever seen around me, or presented as an option – while there were girls in my footy team who were proudly out as lesbians, I was spending most of my time at school, and being gay meant being the subject of ridicule and the butt of jokes. The word 'gay' was used as slang for lame, and it was only acceptable to be bisexual as a punchline in a movie, or in the context of a threesome, which is just a crass over-sexualisation of bisexuality.

In that environment there was no way for me to explore my sexuality safely, and I guess on some level it also scared me to think that I might be different.

In the end, I was saved from making any decisions. One afternoon Teneille arrived at football practice and told me her family was going on holiday to New Zealand for a couple of weeks in the school holidays, and it would be the first time since we'd met that we'd be apart for a decent chunk of time. But before she left, Teneille wrote a letter to me, telling me about how much I meant to her, and confessing that her feelings for me went beyond friendship. That she loved me.

She loved me …

The confusion I felt reading her letter was excruciating. On one hand, I was elated, because I felt exactly the same way; it meant those feelings were real. But on the other, I was twisted with anxiety, guilt and shame – again, I was with Dom. But perhaps more importantly, I didn't know how to define my sexuality, even to myself, let alone to someone else. I just didn't have the words or the confidence to own what I was feeling.

I didn't reply to Teneille's letter. It still pains me to think about it now, the fact that she put herself on the page so vulnerably, and that I never gave her a response. I didn't know what to do, so I did nothing. I stayed with Dom, and tried to push my feelings for Teneille out of my mind.

When she came back from her trip, with her letter still unanswered, we didn't reconnect. I didn't reach out to her, and I can only imagine how she was feeling about it. Thankfully, Teneille would come back into my life again later, but it breaks my heart to remember how paralysed I was by her admission, because if I'd had any idea about how to claim my sexuality, or had even just one single bisexual role model to look up to, perhaps I could have responded with more openness and less shame.

Growing up, I'd struggled with difference all my life, trying to fit in and be 'normal', and another layer of complication just seemed like a bridge too far. I'd spent years trying to downplay the poverty and disadvantage I grew up with, even my Aboriginality, depending on the audience, because it always made it harder to be accepted, despite any of my achievements. So when it came to the powerful feelings I had for Teneille, I don't think I could handle the possibility of being rejected by my friends and family for my sexuality, especially when I didn't understand how to define it myself.

For the last year, Dom and I had been coasting along, and our relationship was just part of the fabric of my daily life, like school, footy and work. Life with Jo was calm and steady, but just like clockwork, I got thrown a curve-ball, and just as I was starting Year 12, I had a pretty bad accident.

Before I left Leanne's to live with Jo, I'd decided to get my moped licence – Dom had a moped and we thought it would be fun if I could drive it too. Soon Dom had bought a new moped, and he loaned me his old one. It was so handy having a mode of transport for myself – especially for getting myself to work and footy training. Leanne had been against it, seeing mopeds as dangerous, and I guess in the end her worries were vindicated.

On this particular night, Dom was at home in Kalgoorlie, and I'd driven the moped from Jo's place to a friend's party. It was a fun night, but I was tired, and as I was leaving, a mate of mine asked if he could get a lift home. Whenever I went out on the moped I made sure to wear the protective gear – jacket and helmet – but for some reason, probably because we weren't going far, this time I gave the gear, including my helmet, to my mate and I jumped on the bike in just the playsuit I was wearing, my arms and legs bare.

The roads were wet that night, and for the first part of the ride, everything was fine. But when I turned the moped to take a corner, the tyres lost their grip, and the moped flew out from under us. We both went sprawling.

My friend was fine, because he was dressed in jeans and jacket, and he was wearing the helmet. But I was pretty banged up with deep grazes on the right side of my body – including the entire side of my face. (To this day, I have slight scar in my eyebrow.) It was a disaster. We weren't far from the party and the crash must have made a big noise, because people came running down the street, including another of my friends, Mason. He picked me up and took me straight to hospital in his ute, where I needed X-rays and had my injuries patched up. Luckily, they were all surface wounds, but in most of my school photos from that year, I was still healing and, the scars and discolouration of my skin are just visible.

When Dom found out, he was really upset, and Jo made it clear in her firm, no-nonsense way that I wouldn't be getting back on a moped ever again. But she agreed that when I finished school later that year, I'd need some transport of my own, so she arranged car driving lessons with an instructor, a lovely older man named Dennis, who I eventually became quite close to. As he gave me driving lessons around the suburbs, we'd talk about what was going on in my life, and before the end of the school year I had my licence.

Those last few months of Year 12 passed quickly, almost too quickly. I felt as I was being pulled along by a force beyond myself, rushing me to the end of an important chapter in my life.

One of the big events in our final year was almost upon us – the Year 12 Ball. Being Head Girl, I was on the organising committee, and bizarrely, we decided on a Winter Wonderland theme, a strange decision for Perth in summer, but I think we were inspired by the proms we saw in American movies. The ball was being held in a church hall near the school, and we spent week after week making beautiful set pieces to decorate the hall with – gumtree branches sprayed with silver glitter, with handmade snowflakes hanging from them with fishing wire.

I had bought a gorgeous dress for the ball on Ebay, and I couldn't wait for it to arrive – buying something online was my only way of finding something affordable with the money I'd saved from work. I was so excited about the prospect of gliding into the hall with Dom on my arm, both of us dressed to the nines, and for the night itself too – a chance to celebrate with all my friends before we entered the real world and worked out our next steps.

But as the date of the ball crept closer and closer, the dress still hadn't arrived, and by the week before the big night, I was a mess.

'I can't afford to buy a new one,' I told Jo, stressing out about my options. Anything I found in store now would be way out of my price range.

'I have an idea,' Jo said, never one to be daunted by a challenge. 'Let's see if we can find a nice second-hand dress.' In an instant she had Gumtree up on her phone, and had typed in a search for 'ballgown' and 'formal dress'.

I was dubious, but as luck would have it, there wasn't one far from us – and it was stunning, a pale lilac, strapless gown with a long flowing skirt and a beautiful sash at the waist. It was more traditional than I'd envisioned for myself, but it was beautiful. I loved it.

'Done,' Jo said, messaging the seller. 'I think you could win "Belle of the Ball" in this!'

In the end, my original dress ended up arriving in the mail the day of the ball, but by then I was so enamoured with the second-hand gown – and trusted Jo's impeccable taste – that's what I wore. Standing in front of the mirror in my bedroom, with my hair up and make-up done to perfection, I felt beautiful.

It was bittersweet, having this milestone happen without my family there. Mum and Nan would have been crying with joy; Mum fiddling with my hair, wanting to change it, no doubt, and Nan shouting for everyone to come and see her Brookey all dressed up and fancy. I felt sad that there was no Eden or Troy to tell me I looked pretty, or joke about how the blokes at the party had better stay in line. No Ky to give me her soft smile, or even Uncle Pinhead to say something silly to cut through all the emotion.

Soon Dom arrived to pick me up, handsome in a black suit and with his hair spiked with gel, as all the boys did back then. Then we drove to the nearby house of a friend, Jessica, where her mum took pre-ball photos taken together, posing out of the front of her house, and then jumped into the limousine we'd hired specially to take us to the ball. I still have the photo of Dom and me together, both looking so young to my eyes now, but it's clear from our shining happy faces that we felt so grown up.

Jo was right – I did win Belle of the Ball, and to celebrate, I danced with Mark Farrell, a friend, who won Beau of the Ball, which was so funny and awkward. We were like brother and sister and we could barely keep a straight face while we danced – I think Dom was even a little jealous watching us, which makes me smile now!

In a way, winning Belle of the Ball was like a final golden touch to what had been an incredible five years of high school for me. It certainly hadn't been smooth sailing – though truly, nothing had been in my life so far. I had been homeless, lost, found again, and somehow had come out the other side, stronger than ever. Now there was the next phase of life to deal with, but I wasn't ready to think about climbing that looming mountain just yet.

That night, I danced with Dom and my friends to the hits that were big at the time – 'Call Me Maybe' by Carly Rae Jepsen, 'One More Night' by Maroon 5 and Nicki Minaj's 'Starships' – with all the energy and excitement of young people on the cusp of adult life. That night, I was just like any other teenage girl, hand in hand with the person she loved, surrounded by friends, and dizzy with happiness. If a stranger had seen me then, they'd have had no idea of what I had been through to get there. But I knew – and I knew that my past was always in my present, and my future was lurking ahead.

Graduation, the final set-piece of my school life, was bittersweet. I won three awards – one for sport, one for leadership, and one for the traineeship program at the hospital I'd taken part in. At a school with a fairly high population of First Nations kids, I was one of only five Aboriginal students to graduate.

I was so proud, walking on stage to accept my Year 12 Certificate, but standing there I was overcome for a moment with the same feeling I'd had accepting my pin as Head Girl. No one else in my family had made it this far in their schooling, and I wished with all my heart my family could see me, especially Troy and RJ. Without them, graduating was a lonely success.

I still have my Year 12 yearbook, with the quote I wrote in it under my photograph. Looking at it now, I'm caught between embarrassment for how cocky I sound, and pride for the tough little thing I was.

I wrote 'A school is only as good as its students. I hope I've made Cecil Andrews a better place.' I love the energy I was sending out, not afraid to own my power!

But I wish I could reach into that photo and shield the optimistic girl I was from what was about to come.

Six

Nothing really prepares you for what life is like in those first months after you graduate high school. You spend over a decade in the system, where everything is laid out for you – someone tells you where to go, where to be, what to do. Even if you have a complicated home life, like I did, there's no expectation beyond just turning up, because the thing you're 'doing' is going to school. Once you graduate though, all bets are off – it's all over to you.

I thrive with a purpose, and for the last five years, mine was to make it to the end of Year 12 and graduate. It had taken all my energy, determination and focus to get there, and so far I'd successfully pushed down the darkness of the trauma of my early life, and the rollercoaster of my teenage life, by keeping myself busy with school, sport, work and my relationships.

But the accumulated stress was always there, simmering in the background, waiting for more fuel to be added to the fire, and for me, that fuel came in the form of leaving the structured world and expectations of school. Soon the stresses and strains of the next stage of my life would slowly turn up the heat, and one revelation in particular would explode life as I knew it.

For the first little while, though, things stayed as they were. After I graduated, I stayed living with Jo; it was my home by then. Most of my mates were finding jobs or starting university in Perth, or heading interstate. Dom and I were still together, and still playing football, and he'd started working at his dad's electrical company in Kalgoorlie.

At the end of my apprenticeship with the antenatal clinic at Armadale Hospital in Year 12, they'd offered me a job to start in the new year. It seemed like a good opportunity to get some steady employment, so I accepted it straight away, even though I was finding the work a bit dull. When you're young, and you haven't grown up with the idea of having big dreams or following your passions, a job is just a job. Now, when I look at social media, I can see that for some of my generation, there's a lot of talk about 'finding your bliss' and making your work fulfilling. It unsettles me, because it's such a privileged way of thinking.

For me, especially then, I had no concept of 'finding my bliss'. I needed income so I could pay my own way – now I was out of school I couldn't expect Jo to look after me forever, and as I was technically an adult I wanted to pay her board, until I was able to cover the rent on a room of my own in a share-house. If had a dream at all, it was to be earning enough to rent an entire house where my brothers and Ky could live with me, maybe back on Nan's country in Quairading.

They seem like such little dreams, now, but for me at eighteen, they seemed aspirational, maybe even a little out of reach.

Jo had other ideas for me, though. When I was finishing my final year at school, she was always talking to me about applying for university courses. I wasn't sold on it, mostly because I didn't

Top left: Nanna, Charlotte Rose Blurton (*back, middle*), with four of her sisters.

Top right: Seanna, my mum, a fierce, staunch blak woman, and my hero.

Below: My family on Troy's first birthday, before RJ was born (*left to right*): Kyandra, Eden, Mum and Troy, me, with Nanna and Uncle Ronald.

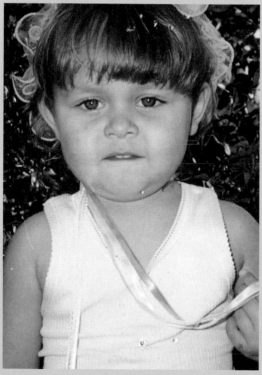

Top left: Me as a baby, about four months old.

Top right, above: The only photo I have of me and Mum together, just us.

Top right, below: With Dad and Leanne.

Bottom left: On my first birthday, staying with Dad and Leanne.

Top left: With baby Troy, after changing his nappy.

Top right: Holding Ky's first baby, Bubba Shane, with my friend Skyla.

Bottom: With Ky, pregnant with Bubba Shane, Mum, and baby RJ.

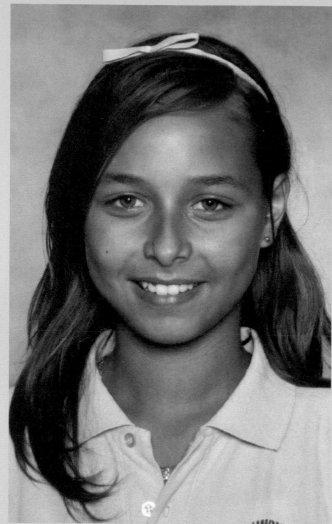

Top left: Starting high school at Cecil Andrews College in Perth, aged twelve.

Top right: My eleventh birthday, at the start of the year that would shake my world.

Bottom left: With Ky, visiting me at Leanne's house.

Bottom right: With Jo, who always gave me the best life advice.

Top: With my team-mates, about to compete in my first State footy championships.

Bottom left: Playing for South Fremantle Football Club.

Bottom right: Playing for the Swan Districts Football Club.

Top left: As Head Girl of Cecil Andrews College, with Mitchell Davies, Head Boy.

Top right: Working for Headspace, the job that fired my passion for youth work.

Bottom left: As Belle of the Ball, with Mark Farrell, Beau of the Ball, at our Year 12 formal.

Opposite, top: At the beach at Quobba Station. This is where Mum swam with sea turtles when she was pregnant with me. Nan was watching and gave me my totem.

Middle left: With RJ at the Pinnacles on our trip to Carnarvon.

Middle right: With Ky in 2021. This was the last time I saw my sister.

Bottom left: With Pete, who's become like a father to me.

Bottom right: With my three brothers, celebrating Christmas (*left to right*): Troy, me, RJ and Eden.

Top left and right: Snapped on the set of *The Bachelorette* by stylist Paul Versace.

Bottom right: Cobar, the man in my life!

find academic work easy, even though I had done OK with my WACE marks, and I'd recently been offered an entry-level business administration role with a big oil and gas company, Woodside. That felt like something I could do – the idea of going to university seemed like a huge, overwhelming thing. What's more, I had no idea what I wanted to study.

'Look, it's about getting started,' Jo told me. 'You just choose something that appeals to you, and give it a go. If you decide to switch degrees down the track, that's no biggie. But you'll have way better options for work if you have a degree. And,' she added with a smile, 'you're so smart, Brooke. Just give it a crack.'

With her help, I collected as many course handbooks and catalogues as I could for the universities in Perth and Western Australia and began flicking through them. She suggested I try sports science, which made sense given my love for footy and all things physical. I applied, and to my surprise I was accepted at the University of Western Australia. I was still playing club football for South Fremantle, and so when I decided to accept the uni place in the new year, I juggled my study along with footy and part-time work at Armadale Hospital.

After my moped accident, I was relying on public transport and lifts from Jo whenever I could snag them – getting to footy training for South Fremantle was a particular trek! – but I knew my life would be so much easier if I had a car. Thanks to the driving lessons Jo arranged for me with Dennis, I had my driver's licence, but there was no way I could afford to buy a car.

It was around this time that Grandma Susette did me an absolute solid, and gave me her old 1990s white Toyota Corolla. In the last six months I'd been catching the bus out to her place in Woodvale to visit her and Troy, and it wasn't an easy trip, though I knew it was important to continue to be there for my little brother.

'Look, it's nothing snazzy,' Susette said to me, as we stood on her driveway looking at the car, 'but it should do the job.'

'Are you kidding?' I gushed. 'It's amazing!'

To me, it was. I *loved* that car. It was my ticket to independence. Susette was always so generous to me, and to my family. Her gift meant the world to me.

From the outside, it might have looked as if life was coming together for me. I had a stable job, I was studying at university, I had a comfortable, loving home, and now I even had my own car. But in truth, I was struggling. I felt lost. Work was dull and repetitive, and I was finding university really tough. Much as I was interested in sport, sports science didn't capture my passion at all – none of the coursework or classes were interesting to me and I was finding it very hard to stay focussed and motivated for my assessments.

University wasn't what I expected it to be. I'd thrived so much with the routine and social structure of school, and I was looking forward to university to fill that void. But the campus was so big and alienating and there were so many students, I found it hard to make friends without the benefit of a clear social scene. University life is designed to be quite independent, and in hindsight I wasn't ready for it. The only saving grace was the Aboriginal Studies department, which I discovered early on – there was a common room where I started hanging out, and I really liked the people I met there, but it didn't have much to do with my actual degree, and I struggled to find the motivation and interest to commit to my studies.

My relationship with Dom wasn't great either. He was busy juggling what was on his own plate – work, football, his family's needs between Perth and Kalgoorlie, and he couldn't be there for me in the way I needed. All my other friends seemed engaged and busy with their new lives, and Teneille, who was on my mind a lot still, had moved on and had a girlfriend. I was lonely and I felt directionless, even though I was still pulling myself together every day and showing up for work and uni.

I was also partying quite bit at that time, though probably not as much as the average eighteen-year-old, fresh out of school. I'd go out with my mates from footy on Friday or Saturday nights, hitting bars and clubs and imbibing in the great Aussie tradition of binge drinking and having a dance. I can't say I enjoyed the drinking part much – I've never been a big drinker, most likely because I've seen the damage that alcohol (and drugs) have wreaked on people around me. But I did always enjoy getting ready before we hit the town – hanging out at someone's house, doing our make-up, laughing and talking before the night really began.

But even though I enjoyed socialising like this, I'd often wake up the following morning feeling hollow and empty, and then the repetitive cycle of the next week would start all over again.

Then, a few things happened that threw everything off balance.

The first was that, once again, I was sexually assaulted.

I've decided not to go into detail about it, but I think it's important to be honest and write about the fact that it happened.

I worry sometimes that in in disclosing my experiences of assault, people may push aside the breadth and complexity of my life and only ever see me as a victim.

Another thing I worry about in disclosing my experiences is that I feel there's an insatiable appetite for personal trauma and an expectation that survivors continuously relive that trauma as a part of our public life, and I don't want to do that. I've worked very hard over a long time in clinical settings to help me come to terms with the assaults I suffered, and sharing the minute details isn't going to help anyone, most of all me. But I do own everything I've been through, and the only thing I want to say about it is that I was assaulted in a context where I should have been able to feel safe.

After it happened, I tried to talk to Dom about what I was feeling, but it was very difficult to express the depths of my trauma, and there was a lot of darkness resurfacing from the assault I'd suffered as a child at Mum's wake, which I'd never been able to process properly in the first place. Dom just wasn't equipped to handle it all, or support me the way I needed to be supported.

I don't have any animosity towards him for this. Like me, he was so young, and it was lot for him to try and understand, on top of all new responsibilities he'd gained since leaving school. And most importantly, we were falling out of love. Instead of my relationship being a source of strength, it fell apart under the pressure of the circumstances, and Dom and I parted ways.

The only bright thing in my stressed and lonely life was football. I'd thrown myself body and soul into training and had made the team again for the State women's footy championships, this time for the Under 23s. The only issue was that the competition would be held in Shepparton, in Victoria. The games would be played round-robin style over a weekend, and the two teams with the most points would go head-to-head in the grand final.

I'd been dreaming about running onto the footy pitch in a final alongside my team for months. I'd trained so hard; I'd thrown everything at it. But it wasn't cheap to get there. All up I needed $2500, which would cover the kit (the uniform and boots), flights to Victoria and the coach to Shepparton, and meals and accommodation. It was money I didn't have yet, so on top of training every other day, I was picking up as many extra shifts as I could at work to get the cash together.

And then, at the worst possible time, I crashed the Corolla. The tyres had been bald for a while, and I'd been procrastinating about getting new ones – but I couldn't afford to replace them *and* keep saving for the footy finals. Every time I got in the car I'd wince – I knew it was dangerous to drive with bald tyres, but I needed to drive to work to earn money, and I needed to drive to get to footy training to stay on the team for the championships.

On this particular day, it had been raining, and all it took was for me to take a corner too sharply. The car spun out and I crashed into a traffic post. Luckily I wasn't hurt, just a little dazed, and the car wasn't badly dented – but now I knew I had to dip into my precious savings and get the tyres fixed. It was ironic – my life was feeling like a car crash, and then it turned into one, literally.

I was feeling low. Lower than when I'd left Leanne's place, lower than when I'd left Dad's caravan, when I felt so winyarn, so bleak and sad. But back then, getting back on track again was more straightforward. School was a constant, and I'd committed to a clear goal of graduating Year 12. But now there didn't seem to be a clear road in front of me – every path I took seemed like a dead end or took me somewhere I didn't want to go.

In the middle of all this chaos, I went to visit Grandma Susette and Troy, and Susette told me some things about Mum, and the night she died.

'Brooke, I didn't tell you this before, because I wanted to wait until you were older,' she began. 'But I think you need to know about this. Your mum came to see me before she died.'

When were in Perth visiting Nan in hospital after her stroke, we were staying with Aunty Brenda, so Mum must have gone on her own to visit Susette.

'She was frazzled, Brooke. I don't think I'd ever seen her like that,' Grandma Susette told me. 'She wasn't herself. Seeing your nan so sick was really taking a toll on her.'

Mum had confided in Susette that she wasn't coping; she was spiralling with dread that her mother was going to die. She told Susette that she didn't believe in her ability to care for us kids without Nan in the picture.

'What are you saying?' I was confused, though I think a part of me knew what Susette was saying.

'I don't know whether your Mum had an accident, or whether she crashed her car on purpose,' Susette said carefully. 'I think she was in a really dark place. I think she may have driven off that night intending not to come home.'

I could barely process the information. When Mum died, I'd been told she'd had a car accident, and while it was sudden and shocking, it had made a lot of sense – she drove a lot, she took a lot of drugs, and she was in a state of unrest when she left me standing in the driveway that day.

But if she'd done it on purpose …

The idea that Mum had taken her own life sent me headlong into a spiral. That she would *choose* to leave us – her children, who had no one else to care for us – it felt selfish, hurtful. How could she have done that to us? Now I understood why everything in my life felt like shit. It could all be traced back to Mum's death.

Until then, whenever I thought of Mum, I felt a deep sadness for her, about her lost potential as a strong blak woman. And in more recent times, hindsight has made me more empathetic to what Mum's thought process might have been at the time. Hindsight has also made me feel a lot for Susette, who had been carrying such a heavy burden.

But hearing that difficult news compacted all the trauma and stress and loneliness I was feeling, and forged it into anger. If Mum had chosen to live, we'd still be together as a family. Yes, life at home had been rough, but family was *everything*. My brothers, my sister, would have been part of my life every day, not just when I could manage to see them. I would have had my people, my community, my culture, surrounding me. There was so much that would have been different.

I tried to work through what it meant to me, but all that would happen was that I'd feel overwhelmed with anger, then hurt and confusion would take its place. I also felt torn – should I tell my brothers, or keep it to myself? When Mum died, Troy and RJ were young enough to have strong positive memories of her, and I didn't want to destroy that now. But my God, it felt lonely keeping it to myself.

My own car crash had left me struggling – I had no idea how I was going to afford the fees for the state championships and get my car fixed.

But somehow, someone was listening to my worries, and help turned up in the form of Dennis, my old driving instructor. We'd stayed in touch since I got my licence, and every so often we'd catch up for a coffee and a yarn. He was such a kind man. He treated me like his daughter or his niece, and took a real interest in what was going on in my life.

One day, not long after my crash, we caught up. The Corolla was still going (just) – and I was still driving it around with bald tyres, which made me anxious.

I drove over to his place to pick him up, and as he climbed into the passenger seat, he said casually, 'Reckon we go get a feed.' Then he directed me to a KFC nearby, where, next door, there was a mechanic.

We parked the car, and Dennis said he was going to say a quick hello to a mate at the mechanics. Soon he was back, and we went and got a feed at the KFC. Dennis and I would talk about everything and nothing – he always just seemed to enjoy the company.

'You're a good kid, Brooke,' he'd say, and I think he really meant it. He could see I was doing my best, but still struggling.

Afterwards, we walked back to my car – where there was a mechanic putting new tyres on the Corrolla.

'What's going on?' I said, confused.

'You needed new tyres. So here they are,' Dennis said, looking pleased as punch.

'Oh Dennis … That's so lovely!' I was flustered – it was one of the kindest things anyone had done for me, but I didn't feel I could accept them without paying him back.

But Dennis wouldn't have a bar of it. 'Just let me do this for you, Brooke,' he insisted. 'I want to.'

The only thing I could do was give him a hug to show him how much it meant to me.

With the tyres sorted out, it meant I could afford to be part of the team for the footy championships in Victoria. I was so excited to be going after all; after living and breathing footy for months, I was going to be bringing my best to the team.

As it happened, Dad had moved to Melbourne in the months beforehand, and we hadn't been in touch lately, so given I'd be flying over, I texted him to let him know about the championships, and invited him to come and watch me play. Not knowing anything much about Victoria, I thought Shepparton and Melbourne were pretty close together. In reality they're a couple of hours apart by car, and so expecting him to drive out to Shepparton was a bit optimistic. But I was so twisted up about Mum and feeling so lost in general, I really wanted to see him; I really *needed* to see him.

Meanwhile, I wasn't getting along very well with my coach.

It doesn't happen often but, every once in a while, I meet someone who I just don't click with, and my coach was one of them. No matter what I did, I seemed to rub her up the wrong way. Perhaps she just didn't like me that much, who knows? Whatever it was, I didn't understand it – to me it seemed as if she thought I needed to be knocked down a few pegs. For instance, at the end of the championships she gave every player in the team a gift, books from the *Little Miss* series, like 'Little Miss Nice' or 'Little Miss Happy'. Mine was 'Little Miss Princess' … not exactly subtle.

Playing in the round robin games on the first day of the comp, I wasn't bringing my best on the pitch. There was so much weighing on my mind, and I was distracted, trying to see if I could spot Dad in the stands, feeling edgy about whether he would make it at all, and whether I'd see him later.

Our team was still doing well though, and after our first two games, we'd made it into the grand final, which would be played the next day. Despite how churned up I was feeling, it was exciting. Maybe Dad would be there in the crowd, watching.

Later that night after a team dinner, we all went back to one of the girls' rooms at the motel, some of us quiet, some chatty and nervous with anticipation about the finals match.

Soon there was a knock on the door and the coach came in. She'd been working out who she'd run in the finals from twenty-two girls – eighteen players and four substitutes, plus the train-ons who'd come along to substitute if one of those twenty-two players was injured.

After chatting with some of the girls, she looked over at me and nodded her head at the door. 'Brooke, can you come outside with me for a sec?' she said. 'Let's have a yarn.'

We walked downstairs to sit in the cool night air on the outside steps.

'Yes, Coach?'

'I've decided not to play you in the finals,' she said firmly.

'What? Are you serious?' I asked, caught between shock and anger.

'This isn't about you, Brooke, it's about the team,' she said. 'You're not on your A-game, so you're on the bench.'

I could barely control my emotions. I felt as if I was going to explode – to scream, or cry. All I could do without bursting into tears or boiling over with anger was nod stiffly and go back to my room, where I finally cried. Later some of the girls came to comfort me and I was grateful for that, but I didn't get much sleep that night.

The next day on the sidelines I dug deep to support my teammates, and cheered our girls on with the others who'd been benched, but on the inside I felt worthless and hollow. It wasn't that I'd never been cut from a team before – I had – it was just that I'd worked so hard to get there. All the hours, all the energy I'd spent training and throwing everything at it; all the time I'd worked; all the money I'd saved. It had been such a grind, but it was all for a purpose – and now it felt like such a waste. I knew I hadn't been playing my best that day, but I honestly thought I would have been an asset on the pitch for the finals.

The rest of the day was a haze of upset and frustration.

Vic Metro won.

Dad never showed up.

The trip home was one of the loneliest journeys I'd ever made.

When I got back to Perth, my mental health started to spiral in earnest. I felt numb, as if there was something getting between me and the world around me, as if my emotions weren't cutting through. Footy wasn't a happy place for me anymore – I felt like a failure – and I stopped playing for a while with South Fremantle, though I still went to the games and cheered them on. Dom was gone, and my mind turned again to Teneille, about the feelings I'd had for her. I began blaming myself for not having the guts to reply to her letter.

My job felt like just a mindless thing I did every day. I'd worked my way into a slightly higher role in the admin team, but it was repetitive and dull. Uni was still filling me with dread, and after six months, I decided I couldn't keep going, and deferred my course. I started worrying about whether I was a burden to Jo, and after work and dinner, I'd retreat to my room, taking refuge in sleep when my mind wasn't buzzing with thoughts and questions.

All the trauma and grief of my past had finally caught up with me. It was swirling around inside me, getting thicker and darker, and I knew that if I gave it a chance to take hold of me, I'd drown. But sometimes, when your mental health is so bad, you reach a point when you don't have the capacity to keep it at bay anymore.

I got to that point. It was the darkest moment in my adult life, and once I was in it, I didn't know how to get myself back out.

I was alone in my room one afternoon, feeling the lowest I'd ever felt. I knew there were people who cared about me, who would listen, Jo especially, but I didn't want to talk to anyone. I didn't want sympathy, I didn't want that kind of support. The only thing I could think to do was get in my car and drive. I drove for hours through the streets of Gosnells, watching the sky grow darker ahead of me, my brain roiling with black thoughts.

Why had my own mother abandoned me, killed herself so that she didn't have to care for me and my siblings? Why did Nan have to die? Why was I assaulted? I was just a kid, didn't I deserve to be safe? Why did everyone I love leave me? Why didn't I have family around me, why was I so alone? What was I doing with my life? I was a failure.

I can't pinpoint when it happened, but all of sudden it entered my mind that I didn't have to live like this. I didn't have to live at all.

Mum had ended it, hadn't she? Mum chose to end all the sadness and the fear and the chaos in her head. In a moment of clarity, I understood her now. It wasn't the 'easy way out', because feeling this low wasn't easy.

I know why you did it, Mum, I thought, tears blurring my vision. *I want to be with you and Nan. I don't want to keep feeling like this.*

I could make the same choice. It felt like the only option.

I drove myself to a railway crossing nearby. I parked across from the tracks, and sat in my car, caught between the overwhelming numbness, and a desire to just make it all stop.

My mind was rushing, full of white noise, and I turned the music up loud in a futile attempt to drown it out. The car felt like a cocoon, keeping me from the outside world, but at the same time it was suffocating. My phone was in my hands, and I was typing messages, incoherent and fraught with emotion. People were dancing in and out of my thoughts, my brain was like a washing machine on repeat.

Mum, Nan, Dom, Leanne, my brothers, Ky, Dad, Jo, Teneille.

Teneille. I typed out a text to her, cryptic but with all the sadness and exhaustion I felt at that moment.

Then I turned the ignition off, clambered out of my car and stumbled for the tracks.

Have you ever been in a city in the middle of the night, when everything feels still even while you can still hear the sound of cars, see the lights of the buildings around you? It's a contradiction, everything right there and yet there's so much quiet. You never feel alone in a city, there's never true solitude. There's always something intruding on your space.

But I was alone that night. On the tracks, I lay back, ignoring the uncomfortable feeling of the metal and gravel beneath my back. I put my headphones in and turned the music up on my phone, as far as it would go. One of Mum's favourites, P. Diddy's 'Missing You'.

Suddenly my phone was ringing. Teneille's name was lighting up the screen. I hit ignore – again, and again, and again, as she kept trying to reach me. I couldn't talk to her. There wasn't a single word I could think of to say to anyone.

My vision was blurring from tears, and I could feel them sliding down my cheeks, trickling at my ears, uncomfortable. An endless loop of sadness ran through my head.

Mum left. Nan died. Why does everyone give up on me?

I didn't really know what death would be – but I knew I wanted the hurt to stop. It was getting closer to morning and the trains would start running soon. I was small, and curled up on those train tracks I wouldn't be visible from a distance.

But before anything could happen, there were lights flashing, the sound of sirens, people yelling. There were police officers standing around me, and voices, questions, everything moving so much faster than I could keep up with.

Later, I found out that Teneille had alerted Jo after she got my messages. She knew something was wrong, that I was in trouble. They called the police, who tracked my phone to find where I was.

Dawn was breaking as they moved me off the tracks. There were no soft words or empathy, and I was bundled into the back of a paddy wagon, like a criminal. I still find it hard to think about that.

But back there in the wagon, I was numb, and I let it all wash over me. I was driven to Armadale Hospital and admitted as an in-patient in the mental health unit.

I was eighteen years old, and alone again. In my hospital room, I curled up on the bed and wished away my life.

Seven

It wasn't the first time I'd tried to take my own life. This memory only returned to me when I started writing my story, but there had been another attempt, much earlier in my life. Too early. Perhaps that's why I'd pushed it down, repressed it under years of other hurt and sadness.

When I was little and our family life was much more itinerant, sometimes Mum would need to take refuge at a women's shelter. This particular memory is from one of our stays in a refuge in Carnarvon, when I was only about six or seven.

I hated staying in those places. If living at home was chaotic, the shelters were mayhem. The staff and volunteers tried their hardest to make them safe, positive places, but if you're housing families of women and kids together who have found themselves homeless or are escaping domestic violence, there's going to be a lot of trauma and damage that comes along for the ride, and it doesn't make for easy living circumstances.

It certainly wasn't easy for Mum, but when she was violent or abusive, especially while we were living in a shelter, I'd be stressed and anxious, waiting for the next bad thing. I felt stuck, caught between Mum being my only real source of comfort and protection, and being the perpetrator of a lot of the worst things in my life.

Behind the building there was a rusty old playground, surrounded by a chain fence. It only had a few bits of equipment, one set of swings and a slide, and there was springy green softfall on the ground, which was prickly and uncomfortable on your bare feet. There were monkey bars, too, and I was playing on them by myself. I'm not sure 'playing' is an accurate way to describe it, because there wasn't any joy in my movements. Back then, I'd spend a lot of my time making wishes, trying as hard as I could to counteract the hollow, sad feeling inside of me, and that day was full of them.

I wish I was rich. I wish Mum wasn't like this. I wish I lived in a big house. I wish I was with Nan. I wish I could die.

As young as I was, somehow I knew that death meant no longer having to live through what I was. There was an old brittle piece of rope hanging loosely over one of the monkey bars – one of those thin, blue plastic ones you use to tie a load down on a trailer – which someone had have left there. It was ancient and stringy, faded by the elements after who knows how long.

And idea formed in my head. Standing on the platform, I tied an end of the rope to one of the rails of the monkey bars, then fashioned a loop out of the other end, making it look like something I thought I could get around my neck. My hands were so small then; I can picture them in front of me, trying to find a way to make the rope stay tied together. Then I put the loop around my neck, and without thinking about it, stepped off the platform. The rope gave way immediately and I thudded to the ground.

Tears were running down my cheeks, the rope loose and scratchy against my throat, the softfall prickling through my T-shirt underneath me. Eventually I got myself up, threw the rope aside and trudged back inside. I didn't tell anyone about it, and I didn't do it again.

It's strange that, more than a decade later, lying in my bed in hospital, I didn't remember my early pain. I'd been admitted to a youth mental health service, the Mead Centre, at Armadale Hospital – ironically, the same hospital as the antenatal clinic I'd been working for. Soon, some of my colleagues would come and visit me, as did many other friends, and I was sometimes overwhelmed with emotion by the kindness of people rallying around me, though at first I felt shame being there and didn't really want anyone to see me in the shape I was in.

But one of the first people to see me was Jo. I felt terrible about what I'd put her through when I went missing that night – she'd seen I was struggling, but I'd just locked myself away in my room, refusing to talk or open up about what I was feeling – and it would have been terrifying for her, trying desperately to find me. She'd invested so much in my well-being, and I felt like I'd let her down. But there she was, ready with unwavering, unconditional love and support as always, the same pragmatic kindness and generosity she'd shown me as a lost teenager, reminding me gently not to be so hard on myself. I was lucky to have her in my life.

For the first little while, I slept a lot. The psychiatrists had started me immediately on antidepressants, which eventually helped me feel more stable, though it was a while before I felt the full effect and it made me feel a bit weird and jittery until then. But in the main, all I felt was exhaustion and I took refuge in sleep, comforted by the break it gave my stressed brain.

Soon, though, as I started to feel more on an even keel, the memory of what had happened that night came back to me in fragments and I felt shocked – frightened even – by how quickly and powerfully those swirling emotions had taken over. Now, with the benefit of some rest and the beginning of the effects of the medication, I knew hospital was the best place for me, and I was relieved to be able to rely on experts and trust the process.

Not long after I was admitted, Dom came to visit. He was quiet and upset, but he had to see me to make sure I was OK. I wasn't up for talking much, but it meant a lot to me that he came. A few other close friends came by, including Teneille, who was relieved to see I was OK; Tess, a close friend who'd I'd met working at Target; and Chelsea, one of my old mates from primary school netball, and her mum, Simone. Another friend, Sam, dropped by as well, a mental health case worker from Carnarvon who I'd met when she'd briefly come across Ky in the course of her work at Graylands. Even Dennis, my driving instructor, came to visit with his wife, which was so touching to me.

And of course Leanne came to see me, which meant a lot. I was so glad to see her. We were family, after all, and she was always there for me when my life was at its absolute worst. It had been a while since we'd spoken last, so it was a little awkward at first – I doubt neither of us expected to be catching up for the first time in a long while in a psych ward.

'I got you these,' Leanne said, pulling out a little stack of books and some colouring pencils from her bag. 'Thought they might help to keep you busy.'

She'd brought me colouring-in books, which were full of all

kinds of beautiful illustrations and patterns to fill in. She'd also brought me some tiny pots of acrylic paint and some art paper so I could do some painting.

'Thanks Leanne,' I said. 'These are so cool.'

The colouring books and paint supplies became a big part of my day-to-day life in the hospital. It was the first time I realised how meditative and soothing art could be for my mind. When I wasn't attending the group sessions and one-on-one counselling, I'd sit in my room for hours, painting, or colouring in, just focussing on the shapes and colours and trying not to think too much about where I was.

Much as I knew I needed to be in hospital – and much as I appreciate how lucky we are in Australia to have access to free mental health services – from my firsthand experience, I don't think the system is necessarily up to the job of tackling the mental health crisis we're seeing around us, especially for young people. Psych wards aren't exactly warm and nurturing places, and the one I was in was no exception. I was in a busy youth in-patient service, with young people aged anywhere from eleven to twenty-five, all at various stages of mental health crises. Every single bed was full.

As I was in immediate recovery, I was in my own room close to the busy nurses' station. There was a common area on the main ward with a TV, but there was only one couch, and uncomfortable plastic chairs and tables, which I hated sitting at. There was a courtyard too, but it was so shady and gloomy I didn't want to spend any time out there. So in the end I spent a lot of time alone in my room.

In-patients had very little agency. Again, I knew hospital was the best place for me, but daily routines like taking medication were policed, and I had to swallow mine in front of a nurse and then open my mouth and move my tongue so they could make sure I wasn't hiding it. Anything that could be considered useful for self-harm was removed – which in my case was my phone charger, so whenever I needed it charged I had to ask the nurses at the front desk.

As days turned into weeks, I began to feel more and more stable, but I had absolutely no appetite and weight was beginning to drop of my already small frame. It wasn't that I was choosing not to eat – the medication I was on made everything look and taste like cardboard to me.

It was such a contrast – before I was admitted I was in peak physical form, having spent months training in the lead-up to the State championships in Victoria. Now I was undernourished and weak, and I was starting to look sickly with dull hair and greyish skin. I guess the body is more connected to the mind than we like to think, because my mental health was having a huge impact on my physical health. But soon the nurses were focussing on helping me to eat properly and my nutrition, and my weight, started to get back on track.

While my experience in hospital was lonely and confronting, it was one of the only times in my life when I'd been able to completely stop and think. When I arrived on the ward, the one question in my mind was, '*How the hell did I end up here?*' and the weeks since had given me the chance to think and regroup. I knew that a lot of what I was dealing with was the unresolved grief and trauma from Mum's death, Nan's passing and the assaults, and there'd never been any time for reflection or to ask for help, because my focus was always on pushing forward, with a hundred per cent of my focus on survival.

I could see now that the goal I'd set of securing my place in the finals team for the championships in Shepparton was ambitious under the circumstances of everything else that was going on for me at the time, and the failure I'd felt was final straw. It was the first time I'd set myself a goal and not been able to make it happen, but I would learn later that it was OK to fail sometimes.

The last thing I wanted was a mental health crisis – I worried that it would be the first step on the same path as Mum, Nan, and Ky. I was determined to get better and make some decisions that would pull me out of the pattern of sadness and depression. I certainly didn't want to end up in hospital again, and I made a promise to myself that I'd always pay attention to the way I was feeling and try to help myself. I'd discover later this was easier said than done, but I knew key to my recovery was to take one day at a time.

After three weeks in care at the hospital, it was time for me to leave – though I wasn't 'recovered', I felt much more on an even keel, and Chelsea and her mum, Simone, immediately suggested that I come and live with them. I didn't want Jo to carry the burden of keeping me on track after hospital – she'd already done so much for me – and soon I was welcomed into their warm family home in South Perth.

Simone was really invested in getting me back on my feet. For the first few weeks, she helped me keep track of my medications, reminded me to take them, and encouraged me to get outside for walks or a run. Simone could always tell when I needed to get out of my own thoughts.

'Let's go and see a movie,' she'd say, cajoling me into getting dressed and heading out. Or she'd take Chelsea and me out for a day at the beach.

Those moments were especially important to my healing. The ocean, the sand, being on country. Nature has always been a powerful remedy for me, and letting the seawater wash over me gave me more strength than anything else in those times.

Pretty soon, it was the start of a new year. I'd just turned nineteen and preseason for footy had started. I knew it was time for me to start playing again. Just like being on country, sport has always been a lifesaver for me, and this time wasn't any different. My teammates – who were also my best friends – would come and pick me up for training from Chelsea's place. Getting back on the field was just what my battered spirit needed. The feeling of adrenaline surging through my body was a tonic for the last few months of forced rest and I was so glad to be back.

Since the disaster of the finals in Shepparton, footy had become a negative space for me, but my team at South Fremantle had always been there for me – they were my safety net. With them I could just reset and remember what I loved about the game, and even more importantly, I could just be myself. For as long as I'd been a part of the team, they accepted me, and celebrated me, and gave me people to lean on, who had no stake in my life except for genuinely wanting me to be well and to feel loved. I was so lucky to have them as a part of my life.

Bit by bit, my life was starting to glue itself back together. Despite how welcoming and caring Chelsea and her family had been, I knew I needed to move on. They'd provided me with a home for that crucial transition period after hospital, but I didn't want to take advantage of their kindness in the long-term, and soon I moved back in with Leanne.

Family is family, and I was grateful there was room for me at her house. The only issue was that I needed to pay rent, and I didn't have a job, but that would change very quickly. Not long after I moved in, Jo reached out to let me know she'd lined up an interview for me with a big mining company, Fortescue Metals Group (FMG), who were in need of a mail room assistant.

I'd never had a job interview before, so I was really nervous showing up on the day at FMG's head office in the city. It was a big step up from handing out resumes at the local shopping centre! Despite feeling churned up on the inside, I must have shown more confidence than I realised, because I got the job. It seemed that Donna, the woman who recruited me, and I just clicked from the very beginning. After a few weeks in the role, I asked her why'd she'd hired me from the raft of other candidates.

'You know what? I don't actually know how to explain it,' she said. 'But from the moment I met you, there was something inside me, saying "Pick her". It just felt right.'

It felt right for me, too. Once again, I took the job that was offered to me and dedicated myself to it. Now, I can confirm that – hand on heart – that I was *not* following my bliss all the way to FMG's mailroom, but in a strange way I did find a kind of joy there. While the work wasn't particularly challenging – my role was to manage the mail room, keep things neat and tidy, oversee the daily post and deliver it to my colleagues – I was doing it well, and the daily routine of going to work really helped my mental health. I began to thrive. Compared to the lack of structure and direction I felt at university, my work was giving me clear and immediate outcomes, whether it was cash in my bank account, or just finishing a task and knowing I'd done it exactly right.

Working for a mining company as a First Nations person felt quite conflicting at times. At that age, I wasn't very politically engaged, but I understood enough that the industry I was working for was often guilty of destroying precious country and not making proper reparations with traditional owners. So while I was always committed to doing a good job, at a deeper level I wasn't particularly invested in the success of the company and their goals because of mining's impact on our land. But I guess when you're forced to engage with a system that was built on the violent dispossession of your people, you learn how to come to terms with that kind of contradiction.

Between footy and work, I was starting to feel like myself again, and now that I had a regular pay packet, I could afford to live somewhere that was truly my own. I really appreciated Leanne giving me somewhere to stay again, but it was time for me to go.

At first, I wanted to find somewhere just for me. I'd never lived alone before, or had any control over my living environment, and I loved the idea of having a little flat to myself, one I'd decorate and keep tidy and organised. But I quickly found out that was a pipe dream – weekly rents for one-bedroom apartments were way out of my budget. I needed to find a suitable share-house, so I put the word out with my friends and eventually I found my first house through a casual acquaintance whose friends were looking for a housemate.

The three guys I moved in with were all true blue blokes – friendly, boisterous and cheerful tradies, who all drove dirt-bikes, and one of them had a girlfriend who also lived with us. The house in Morley was pretty basic but it was cheap, and it was comfortable, and I had space to myself and company whenever I needed it – everything I'd been looking for. The guys treated me like a little sister, which was a bit of a relief. Having never been shy of male attention myself, the only concern I had about moving in with so many guys was whether one of them would try it on with me, but they were all really respectful, and I loved living there.

I'd never owned any furniture of my own, so I made my first-ever trip to IKEA, which felt like a rite of passage in itself. It was exciting cramming my choices into the back of my battered old Corolla and putting it all together when I got home. I can't say that the doors on my new wardrobe opened perfectly every time, but as I surveyed my room with its new bed and cupboards, I was so proud of having done it all on my own.

Soon I had a really good routine going. Being active felt great as a start to my day so I'd get up early when the sun was rising, and hit the gym. Then I'd go into work, and afterwards I'd head off for footy training, or catch up with friends or the guys at home. With the help of my doctor, I also started weaning myself off the medication I was on.

At work, Donna was beginning to realise that I wasn't just a pretty face and kept me busy with extra tasks. Then she offered me a new role, on reception, where I'd be managing calls and visitors at the busy front desk. At first I was keen for the change. I enjoyed the work in the mail room but there wasn't much more to learn, so I figured reception would give me some new skills.

Around the same time, my share house with the tradies split up, and I moved to another house which was technically also a share-house, but my housemates were fly-in-fly-out (FIFO) mine workers and were barely ever there. Most of the time I had the whole place to myself, which was fine, but it meant I was a little lonely.

Eventually the mine workers moved out and I took over the lease. Soon I'd invited Ronnie, a good friend from footy, to move in, and it was really cool living with a mate. Since Teneille had visited me in hospital, she and I had reconnected as friends, and she was flourishing in her life, out and proud with a new girlfriend. Soon she moved in, too, and living with her and Ronnie was the most fun I've ever had in a share-house. We would cook and eat together, and host parties, and we turned the garage into a 'girls cave', complete with a ping-pong table, which became like a little refuge from the world.

It was around this time that I had my first serious relationship with a girl. I'd been dating a guy in recent months, but he was getting a little possessive so I ended it, and then, one night, when I was out clubbing with my football mates, I met Tara.

For me, it was love at first sight.

In a way, I don't think anything would have happened with Tara that night if I hadn't been surrounded by the friends I was with then. That community of women from footy accepted me completely and I felt safe to be myself – the real Brooke. Me being Indigenous was something that was unique and special about me, not a way to stereotype me or keep me down. Perhaps more importantly, loads of the girls I played footy with had come out and were gay, and were proud to be. Lesbian relationships were completely normal, so the night I met Tara was the first time I felt I could act on the feelings I was experiencing for a girl.

The Court, a gay pub in the city and one of our favourite places to go, was absolutely pumping that night. It was such a fun, chilled out place – you could always find people to hang out with and have a good time.

From the moment I saw Tara that night, I couldn't keep my eyes off her. She played footy for another club, and we'd occasionally played against each other, but I'd never seen her like this before – she was dancing, and she just looked so free and beautiful. Eventually, with the encouragement of my mates, I got the courage up to say hello – and for the next seven or eight months we were inseparable. It wasn't long before she moved in with me, with Ronnie and Teneille. I was besotted; I wanted to spend every spare minute I had with her.

Ultimately, being with Tara was how I came out to a lot of people. Because I was part of such an open and accepting community, no one batted an eyelid, and that was that. Beyond my circle of friends, I didn't feel the need to come out officially either – being with Tara felt natural and normal, and for the first time in a long time, I was starting to feel a lot happier with who I was, and a lot more comfortable about my sexuality.

I remember taking Tara to a regular family barbecue at Leanne's folks' house – Maureen and Baz meant a lot to me; they always treated me as part of the family and I considered them grandparents.

When we were leaving, someone said, 'Oh, it's so nice to meet your friend, Brooke.'

'Actually,' I said, 'she's my girlfriend.'

And just like that, I was out. Over the years, I've thought a lot about my 'coming out', because people often ask me about it, expecting more of a story. The reality is that there weren't many people in my life to come out to.

A lot of coming out stories go one way: young queer people face their loved ones and risk being turned away and being ostracised. For many, many people, that bearing of the heart and soul is painful and traumatic; I've seen it a lot in the lives of young people I've worked with. But that bearing of the soul can also be a site of love. For many people, showing their true authentic selves to the people they care about is a chance to be accepted and celebrated and shown the unconditional love they deserve.

I didn't have the pain and trauma of a bad coming out. But equally, I didn't ever get to experience the joy and love of a good one with close family, and that makes me feel sad sometimes.

Paradoxically, another side of being in a same-sex relationship with Tara was that lots of people, especially my footy mates, misread me as being a lesbian – almost as if the relationships I'd had with men were chalked up to me having been in the closet. The truth is, gender simply isn't a factor in terms of who I love.

But having finally found the courage to be in an out-and-proud relationship with a woman, I didn't want to rock the boat by correcting people and pointing out that I was bisexual, something that I now personally understood about myself. And so began the ongoing pressure I felt to identify as gay with my gay friends, and as straight with my straight friends. It seemed there still wasn't a place for me to exist as just Brooke, open to the love of any gender expression.

It would be a while before I had the words or the confidence to express myself like I have in this book.

Life was good. I had a loving home-life and supportive friends, steady work, and my mental health was feeling far less precarious than it had been a year before when I'd been hospitalised. I wasn't one hundred per cent 'better', but I was looking after myself and I felt as if I was coping really well, juggling all the elements in my busy life.

At work, I wasn't loving the reception role, and Donna was keen to keep me on, so she found me an administration role, working in facilities management and arranging travel. I liked the change, and I got to learn more desktop skills, which I knew would help me in my future work life, and give me more options in terms of future employment. With Jo's voice in my head, I was always thinking a few steps ahead and what I might need in my skills toolkit.

But almost as soon as I'd planted my feet under my new desk, my role was made redundant. I'd known for a while that cuts were being made around the office, but I hadn't expected to be in the firing line, so when I was called into a meeting with my new supervisor, I was totally blindsided.

'We're really sorry Brooke,' she said. 'You've been a great asset, but we have to let you go.'

Worse, the company's redundancy policy meant that I had to pack up my desk and leave straight away.

As I left the building, I was a mess. I'd worked there for a little over a year and I was finally feeling secure and relaxed. It couldn't have been worse timing, because I'd just taken out a loan to get a new car – my poor old Corolla had finally given up the ghost – and I'd felt confident and secure enough in my work to go into debt for the first time.

Now I had bills to pay as well as my rent, and no job.

I spiralled again. Walls felt like they were closing in, and I let them. When I got home I barricaded myself in my bedroom for days, and stayed in bed. I felt so overwhelmed, I couldn't even do little things, like get up or go for a run. I just wanted to close my eyes and make it all go away, or at least just keep it all at bay for a while.

Then Tara and I broke up. I was dealing with my own demons, and it didn't seem fair to pull her along for the ride with me. How could I be a present partner when my mental health was deteriorating? But it also meant I'd lost another vital element of support and security in my life. Soon my mind was swirling with endless circular thoughts and questions: No job, payments due. What was I doing with my life? Would anything ever be easy? Why was I so alone? I was so sick of having life knocking the wind out of me.

I knew I needed to start looking for another job, but even just opening an internet browser felt impossible. That's the thing about depression, everything and anything feels insurmountable. And it was hard in moments like this to prevent my thoughts from getting darker, to swirl around Mum and her suicide.

I didn't always think about it consciously, but the fear of ending up like Mum, or Ky, was always with me. It felt like no matter how hard I tried, I kept finding myself at a crossroads, where I could make the choice to just let go and find myself where they had been.

I got it then: why Mum chose drugs, why she lived so vicariously. The other way was so much harder. Working, grinding, struggling every day, and still barely making it. Maybe it would be easier to just let it all go, give up. But this time there was something holding me back – I couldn't choose to act, but I equally couldn't give up. I was stuck. That bedroom became my sanctuary while my thoughts kept chasing their tails.

My saving grace was Ronnie. She'd started worrying about the way I was behaving, and found Leanne's number, then gave her a call.

I was in bed, hiding under my doona, when she arrived. I heard voices and then a sharp rap on the door.

'Brooke, it's me,' she said, her voice all matter-of-fact like it was when she was solving a problem.

I didn't respond. I just squeezed my eyes shut even tighter.

'Brooke, come on, you gotta get up. This isn't good,' she said. 'Open the door and we can have a chat. You've gotta eat and shower, and then you'll feel a bit better. Or do you need me to take you back to the hospital?'

I didn't want to be back in that place again. I felt dread in my bones just thinking about it. I started crying.

'Because if you're like this, you need help, Brooke,' Leanne kept talking.

I forced myself to get up, my body stiff and sore from not being used. I shuffled to the door, then opened it. I wasn't able to look at Leanne, but I felt her pull me into a hug, and I sobbed.

'Come on,' Leanne said into my shoulder. 'Let's get you fixed up.'

With Leanne's help, I got myself decent, and she drove me to the hospital. I watched the streets slide past the window in the car, and for the first time since I was made redundant, I felt a little less hopeless. At the hospital, I had a consultation with the doctors. We agreed that I'd stay overnight in the mental health unit, and the next day we worked up a care plan and I was prescribed more antidepressants.

Leanne picked me up and drove me back home, and Ronnie and Teneille were ready with help and support. It took a while for the medication to hit my system, but soon I started a little feeling better, although I was still anxious about not having a job. There were still bills to pay, and I didn't want to let down my flatmates with the rent or default on my loan.

I started using a mantra: *Just get through this one day – don't worry about the next one. Just one day.* I focussed on each hour as it came, and made my goals small, and it helped me to not feel overwhelmed. *Get up, eat breakfast, have a shower, go to the gym.*

For a while, my world became quite small, and hour by hour, day by day, I held to my goals. I also started researching depression and holistic approaches to managing mental health, and the sense of hopefulness became stronger every day. While I'd come close to the edge, I hadn't fallen into the hole this time, and I knew that was a big win.

Soon I was able to concentrate on looking for work online, and on a whim I put a post on Facebook, saying that I was looking for work if anyone knew of anything.

A few hours later, an old friend messaged me. Ingrid was another footy friend, and I'd always found her interesting and inspirational. She'd been through a lot in her life, too, so in a way we understood each other, and she owned her own Indigenous consultancy connecting mob with work opportunities.

'Hey Brooke,' she wrote. 'I saw a job going at Headspace that might suit you! They do mental health stuff, they're really cool.'

We chatted, and I found out more about Headspace and the job. Their focus on mental health support for young people was something I found really fascinating and important. The job itself was combined reception–administration role, which I now had experience in, but I wasn't sure if my skills would translate exactly. When I looked the job up on the Headspace website, I fought every ounce of imposter syndrome, crossed my fingers and applied for it.

You could say I was very surprised when I got the call for an interview soon after. I got myself ready and drove all the way to the other side of town to the Headspace offices, all the while pushing negative thoughts out of my head, imagined reasons why they couldn't possibly choose me for the job.

In the interview, I was nervous, but I was also professional and determined to do my best, and luckily none of the questions made me stumble or reach for an answer. Soon the recruitment manager and I were nearing the end of the interview, and there was one last question.

'Tell me, Brooke, why do you want this role?'

I paused for a second. I knew there was a stock standard response to this question – I was meant to yarn about how much I wanted the opportunity to be part of the organisation, and how I was passionate about their work and their programs.

I chose to be honest.

'Truly?' I said. 'I really need a job. I'm on my own, and I don't have family to support me, and I just got made redundant. So right now, I would take any job,' I stopped, and took a deep breath. 'But I also think the work you do is really cool. I've battled a lot with my own mental health, and I know the impact your programs would have had on me, if I'd been able to connect with you guys. So yeah, I need the job, but I also think I could bring something from my experience to your organisation.'

Some people like to say everything happens for a reason. I don't think I ever understood what that meant, because there have been a lot of bad things that have happened in my life, and none of them brought any good along with them. But when I got the call from Headspace telling me that I'd got the job, it was one of those moments that showed the truth of that idea.

I think I *was* meant to get that job at Headspace because, without a shadow of a doubt, it was the first step that led me to where I am now.

At first, I just thought of it as just another reception job, but it would become much more than that. The organisation had an extraordinary culture of passion, hard work and respect, and every single person cared about their work – to them it was more than a job, it was a calling. It was exciting to be there every day, watching how they made a difference in people's lives. Most of my colleagues delivered programs with young people, helping them manage their mental health, school and home life, or did important advocacy work helping make mental health a priority in people's lives. My colleagues would send around articles about breakthrough mental health research and new services or programs for young people needing support, which I found really interesting.

But most empowering of all, the people I worked with wanted to know what I thought about their programs – they wanted my input, and they valued my ideas and opinions.

It lit a fire in me.

I knew so much about the work they were doing, because I had experienced a lot of the problems they were hoping to change. It was exciting to be in the hub of conversation and action to address youth mental health crises, when I had always felt so alone dealing with my own. I started to think perhaps there was a career path for me after all, something that was much more than just a job I turned up to every day.

The rest of the team at Headspace cottoned on pretty quickly that I had more to offer beyond answering the phones and helping with admin. With my manager's support, my colleagues began asking for my help whenever they needed an extra pair of hands for a program, or they'd invite me to come along when they were giving presentations at schools or at public health summits. I loved it.

But most of all I loved getting to know the young people who were taking part in the programs. I'd make a point of saying hello to everyone and banter with the chatty kids. Soon I started to see the progress they were making. It was so rewarding watching them transform, and I began to ponder how I might be able to transition into youth work myself. As I watched my colleagues work with the kids, I could see it was a combination of being a good communicator, connecting and engaging with young people, and coordinating and organising activities. I knew I could all those things in a heartbeat, but I still wasn't feeling very confident about my skills in this new environment.

The real tipping point came when Headspace hosted celebrations for its ten year anniversary. Over the six or seven months that I'd been there, my workmates had all come to know me better, and had learned bits and pieces about me and my experiences.

I guess they must have figured there was a lot more to me than met the eye, because my manager asked me to share my story as part of the program for the anniversary event. I was surprised to be asked, and happy to do it, and the night before I wrote out a bit of a speech.

It was a pretty low-key affair held in the office, with some of our associates from other not-for-profit metal health organisations, and representatives from some of our broader networks, like RUOK, who I would eventually become an ambassador for. Even though I hadn't done much public speaking since leaving school, I still felt confident in front of a crowd, but as I stood there listening to the other speakers before me, I started feeling a little nervous, mostly because I didn't think there was much in my story that would be of interest.

Soon the MC introduced me. 'We're excited to hear from a member of our team today, a remarkable young woman, Brooke Blurton.'

I made my way to the front of the room, and as I stood at the podium, I felt a little shiver ran up my spine at the prospect of their undivided attention for the next few minutes.

'Well,' I started. 'I'm going to start at the beginning.'

I told them about my family. How Mum was a fiery, brilliant woman whose life was ruined and then cut short by drugs and poverty and mental illness. How Nan died too soon, because, thanks to the trauma we've suffered over generations, mob have so much lower life expectancies than white Australians. I told them about being split from my siblings, and always knowing the feeling of being hungry. About being homeless at sixteen, and how alone I felt at that time. I even told them about my suicide attempt, the lowest I have ever felt in my life.

I spoke honestly, from the heart, and when I finished, the room was so quiet you could have heard a pin drop. I looked at the people in front of me – colleagues, friends, strangers. They looked completely gobsmacked.

For a moment, I didn't know what to think. It was strange to see how struck everyone was by what I'd told them. I guess when you're living with the daily reality of trauma, of dispossession and disenfranchisement, it doesn't feel remarkable at all. It feels ugly and banal, embarrassing and shameful. I'd always wished for a normal life. But in that moment, I realised that there was power in my story.

I could articulate the nuances of complex and intergenerational trauma and why those things happen, and I could also show organisations like Headspace what they could do to help. I could speak openly and candidly about my experiences and point out where the gaps were in the system, and services. I could offer my experiences as young person as powerful learning tools which could help improve and tranform programs and approaches. I could demonstrate that listening to young people and inviting them as partners in the design of services was crucial.

I realised how far I'd come. That I'd escaped my circumstances – because I was standing in a room of people who would never have guessed where or what I had come from. But I also realised that I had a purpose, and that was to help young people like me to feel less alone. Looking around the room, I could see how much of an impact my story had on the adults in front of me – and then I imagined the impact it could have on a young person.

I realised then and there what it was that I wanted to do: I wanted to work in suicide prevention, with young people, and especially with Aboriginal and Torres Strait Islander people.

That evening, I had so many people wanting to talk to me I could barely get a moment to sip a glass of water. I could see there was a newfound respect in their eyes, as if they could see me for who I really was – more than just the receptionist, someone who had survived and who had so much to offer.

One of the senior managers came to chat to me.

'Have you ever thought about going into youth work?' he asked.

'Yes,' I told him eagerly. 'I think it's exactly what I want to do.'

'Well, we should talk then,' he said.

I felt like my heart was swelling up with pride. I wished I could have shared that moment with Mum or Nan, or Ky, Eden or Troy. I've found that I always grieve the loss of my family the most in happy moments, not sad ones.

The following week, I enrolled myself into a Diploma of Youth Work with TAFE WA with the full support of Headspace, who would cover the costs of my study and assist with the necessary work-placement hours to complete the course. For the first time in my life I could see a strong and purposeful future – and even better, I was already on my way. Soon, with the help of my managers, I started stepping more and more into hands-on community-based youth programs, and really thrived in it.

Around the same time, a few friends tagged me in Facebook posts about the 2016 Miss NAIDOC Perth program. It had just been announced and they were encouraging me to nominate myself.

The six-week leadership and development program is for young Perth-based Aboriginal and Torres Strait Islander women under thirty, and the winner goes on to be an ambassador for NAIDOC events for that year. If you get in, you take part in workshops that focus on developing leadership and communication skills, like public speaking, but there's also a fun professional photoshoot, and cultural activities with Elders, with the winner announced at a big flashy finale event.

It might sound like a beauty pageant, but it's the furthest thing from one as you can imagine. In our First Nations culture, there's a strong tradition of women as the first educators, who share knowledge of culture and mob with younger generations. And this is what Miss NAIDOC celebrates – that women have powerful agency and contribute to the longevity and survival of our culture. Ultimately the program focus is on honouring cultural knowledge and history, building strong relationships and using those skills to be better leaders in the community.

One of the sad things for mob is that through invasion, our families being torn apart, and the injustices we still face today, a lot of our culture and traditions have been torn apart. I feel sad that I don't know more language, and that I don't have a stronger understanding of how my people cared for and continue to care for country, the rituals and practices that were passed down generations. Nan gave us what she could, but she didn't have that immersion either, and this is exactly what Miss NAIDOC aims to address in part – to help fill some of those gaps in our knowledge as young First Nations women, and help lift us up as future leaders and educators in our communities.

I decided to give it a go. *What do I have to lose?* I thought, channeling a bit of Jo's energy as I completed the online application. It was exciting when I heard I'd made it into the program, and I enjoyed meeting the twenty-three other young Aboriginal women who were participating alongside me in the activities and workshops. We came from all walks of life and backgrounds – some were youth or community workers like me, others worked in the arts, or in medical or legal professions, and some were mums – we were all there to proudly represent and celebrate our communities.

When the finals came around, I invited Eden and Troy to come to the fancy crowning ceremony and finale dinner with me at the Crown casino. When they both arrived, all scrubbed up and in collared shirts for the night, I was so proud – my brothers had turned into strapping, handsome young men and I loved showing them off. I wore a beautiful red dress, and I felt gorgeous in it.

The ballroom was absolutely pumping that night, filled to the brim with Aboriginal and Torres Strait Islander people – all the young women involved in the program and their families and friends. The atmosphere was incredible – I'd never been to a First Nations gathering of this size before and it was magical to see so many people who looked exactly like me and my family there. In fact, there were lots of people there who knew the Blurton mob – more than a couple of times people approached me to ask me if I was Charlotte Blurton's grand-daughter, and it was great catching up with this extended network who all knew my beautiful nanna.

While it was a great night, unfortunately the event didn't end so well for me. Up on stage, each of the participants was asked to answer a question from the judging panel, and mine was 'Tell us what reconciliation means to you, why it's important, and how we can achieve it'.

Standing there under the lights on stage, I froze. There were three parts to the question, and I didn't know where to start; it felt too complicated. My tongue felt clumsy in my mouth and I quickly garbled something, then raced off the stage as fast as I could, hot with embarrassment. It was moments like this when I felt like my childhood and circumstances really came to the fore – I hadn't grown up discussing ideas like reconciliation around the dinner table with educated parents, though I'd certainly lived through enough circumstance to know it's crucial if our mob is going to survive for another hundred thousand years. But that night on stage, I simply didn't have the vocabulary.

I wasn't going to let it ruin my night or the fantastic experience I'd had with the program, though. I shook it off and clapped and cheered for the winner, who thoroughly deserved the title – a really impressive young Wiilman-Noongar woman, Shelley Cable, who was kicking all kinds of goals as a finance analyst. Eden and Troy cheered me up, told me I was hot, and I took solace in just having my gorgeous brothers there supporting me.

I often look back to that night and think about how far I've come. Working on TV, radio and social media, public speaking feels like second nature to me now. Even more so, I've learned how to codeswitch, between 'public' life and my own, adapting the different parts of my history and identity for different audiences. I have a different vocabulary, a different tone of voice, even a different accent, especially when I'm engaging with more of a 'white', mainstream audience. I guess I figured out early on that if I spoke like the blak girl I am, who grew up in poverty in rural Australia, maybe people would dismiss me more easily.

'You sound like a whitefella,' I've had cousins say to me before. 'Imagine if you went full blackfella on all them TV people?'

And then we laugh, because people would think I'd had a brain transplant!

I don't think codeswitching is necessarily a good thing – I hate that I need to actively downplay my heritage and my past in order to be invited and accepted in mainstream society. It's just another reflection of prejudice and inequality at when it comes to race, class and education. But it's been an invaluable tool for me, as it is for other people I know who've also made that leap from a struggling past to a more public present.

That night at Miss NAIDOC, I resolved to take more opportunities to develop my confidence – it was scary to put myself forward like that, but it was exhilarating to be a voice for my mob. And later, that would be the very reason why I ended up on television.

Now that my mental health was back on more of an even keel, I was dating again, and was in a fairly serious relationship with another girl, Sally, who I'd met through footy. Sally was just a beautiful human being, the kind of person everyone loves because they're a genuinely good person.

True to form, I fell head over heels, and Sally and I moved in together within a few months of dating. What can I say? When I love a woman, I have no brakes! In the gay community this is known as being a U-haul lesbian – committing quickly to a relationship and moving in soon after the first date.

Sally was a few years older than me, and her maturity and self-confidence opened me up to some great new experiences. The year we were together, we booked a trip to Bali for Valentine's Day, and hand on heart, that was truly the first 'boujie' thing I ever did. For someone who'd spent their childhood scrounging for food and picking nits out of their hair, it was exciting to be booking flights for my first ever overseas trip for no other reason except to sip cocktails and enjoy myself. It was also the first holiday I was sharing with a partner, and the first time I'd spent my hard-earned money on anything resembling self-care. If I needed a sign that life was kicking up a notch, this was it!

Unfortunately, no one passed the memo along to Bali, because I spent half the trip miserable, struck down with 'Bali belly', food poisoning that kept me out of the pool and next to the toilet for a while. Sally was in a bad way, too, and the whole ordeal was tricky for me as I have a phobia of vomiting. Thanks to the work I've done with counsellors, I know it's related to the challenges of my childhood, hearing people like Uncle Pinhead retching in the morning after a big night on the booze.

While I genuinely loved Sally, we broke up soon after we returned from Bali. The enforced rest on holidays had given me time to think, and it had begun to slowly dawn on me that I was still doing what I'd always done – running on a treadmill of busyness, an endless loop of distraction, and until recently, rushing from crisis to crisis. When I wasn't working, I was filling every other moment of my time exercising or with the person I was in love with, filling up my time and space so that I didn't have time to think.

It was swiftly becoming clear that what I actually needed was to be alone and navigate life on my own for a while. Being with Sally was one of the best relationships of my life, and in the future it would be a benchmark for what a respectful and loving relationship was – but I needed to spend some time by myself and focus one hundred per cent on my healing so that I wouldn't end up spiralling again when life threw me curveballs. I wasn't naive enough to think there wouldn't be more challenges ahead, and I couldn't rely on other people to catch me. I needed to be able to do that for myself.

So, single and secure for the first time in my life, it was time to think about my next steps. I had a feeling that there was a big change ahead.

Eight

'I think I'm going to move to Sydney,' I told Jo.

Jo raised her eyebrows, reacting in the typically understated way she did to any big news.

She'd invited me out for a catch-up and a coffee at a local café. I'd been offered an amazing job in Sydney with AFL SportReady, a role that supported young people through education and training with the goal of employment in sports related industries.

When I received the call from Andrew, the manager of SportsReady, offering me the job, I thought it was a sign. Young people and footy – my two passions in one job! But once the excitement at getting the job had worn off, worry had set in. I would have to pack up my whole life and move all the way across the country. Apart from all the logistical arrangements, which would be a lot to deal with on their own, I also had to contend with the fact that I'd be moving away from my family.

I was feeling stressed and uncertain, so I messaged Jo. She invited me out for a coffee, and as I walked into the café, seeing her familiar face gave me an immediate sense of relief. I knew she'd give me some wise advice, as she always did.

For a while, I'd been feeling restless in Perth. I loved working at Headspace – I'd finished my Diploma of Youth Work and was assisting in youth focussed community engagement programs. But I was always thinking about how I could challenge myself to learn and achieve more to become a fully fledged youth worker. I loved working directly with young people – because of my own experiences, I often knew exactly what they were going through and feeling. I'd definitely found my calling.

I'd lived in Western Australia all my life, and in Perth ever since I'd arrived at Leanne's house as an eleven-year-old. Living close to country was important to me, but I was also aware that there was a whole other part of Australia – a huge part – that I knew nothing about. While I'm a WA girl through and through forever, I think people living on the west coast sometimes suffer from a bit of cultural cringe, as if we haven't 'made' it until you crack the east coast. I've definitely grown out of that now, but at twenty-one, I was beginning to dream of what else might be out there for me.

So I'd started keeping an eye out for jobs that looked interesting in Sydney and Melbourne, and that's when I saw a role come up with AFL SportsReady. I'd sent in my application, and had been feeling pretty uncertain about it. It felt like a long shot, but I wanted to give it a go – and I could think of many, many times in my life when my doubts had been proven wrong, so I knew it was worth trying. I was thrilled that I got an interview, and excited when I was offered the role.

Weighing on my mind was that I didn't see my brothers or Ky nearly as often as I wanted to, especially Ky. I was in regular contact with Eden, who was now twenty-five and living in Karratha with his beautiful partner, Jacqui; and Troy, who was seventeen, living with his best friend's family in Perth and training as a car glazier. I knew RJ was OK in Carnarvon with his Dad, and was doing well at high school. But me being in Perth meant I knew I could be there for them all in a flash if they needed me. The proximity was a blessing. A move to Sydney would mean there'd be thousands of kilometres between us, the breadth of an entire continent. If something went wrong, it could take up to two days to get to them, and that was a scary thought.

Now I had a big decision to make. Was I really going to move to the other side of the country?

'So, what's going on with you?' Jo asked, once we'd ordered our coffees.

I told her about the job, and about how restless I'd been feeling lately.

'Go for it, Brookey,' she said, smiling. 'You've gotta take these risks in life, that's how you keep moving forward. The worst thing that can happen is that you move back home.'

She was right, but there was also the risk of leaving a good job at Headspace for the unknown. I knew what it was like to feel financially stressed, but the feeling in me that I needed change was strong.

'What does the family say?' Jo asked.

'They think I should give it go,' I said, shrugging. Eden and Troy had both responded in exactly the positive, chilled out way I'd expected. They always supported me doing what I wanted, but I still felt anxious about being away from them. Ky was harder to track down, in fact, most of the time I had no idea where she was, but I know she would have encouraged me to go too.

'Then I guess you know what the answer is,' Jo said. 'It always feels uncomfortable putting yourself out there or taking a risk, but you can't live life being afraid to do anything all the time.'

Jo always knew what to say. I left the café still a little nervous, but now I was certain in my decision. I would go.

The job would start soon, so I launched myself into action and the rest of my time in Perth was a whirlwind. I broke the news that I was moving to Ronnie and Tenielle, and listed my few precious pieces of furniture on Gumtree to sell. Then I crammed the rest of my life into two big black suitcases, rolling every piece of clothing I owned into a tight little bundle so I could fit as much in as possible.

It was bittersweet leaving the house I shared with Ronnie and Teneille. I'd loved living with them so much – they'd been so supportive of me, through thick and thin, and we'd created some very happy memories together as housemates. They were both excited for me and my move to Sydney, but we all knew life wouldn't be the same again.

After farewell drinks on my last night in Perth, it felt surreal sitting in the back of a taxi on my way to the airport to catch the midnight red-eye flight to Sydney. I had no idea when I'd be back. As the plane lifted off the runway, I felt a twinge of sadness, but I thrust it aside and focussed on the prospect of my new life in a new city.

I arrived in the early hours of the morning, and went straight to my friend Rob's place in Zetland, in south Sydney. Rob and I had met at my gym in Perth – he'd recently moved to Sydney and had kindly offered to let me stay with him until I found my own place. It was only a few days later that I started in my new job, and I jumped in feet first.

My work involved mentoring and supporting young people who were either at school or who had already left – the focus of the program was to assist them in education or traineeship programs associated with the sport industries to create pathways into work and careers. Again there was so much that I understood about this kind of program as I'd taken part in one myself at high school with the antenatal clinic at Armadale Hospital, and the skills I'd learned there had really helped me.

I loved the ethos that Andrew, my boss, had instilled in the organisation at SportReady – as a First Nations man himself he knew how important it was to have a diverse team, and the people running the programs were mostly young Indigenous women like me. My role was a combination of mentoring and administration, more often than not with Indigenous kids, checking in with them to see how they were progressing and helping them with any support they might need to stay on track, and recording their progress through the program. It was an interesting job, combining the two things I was passionate about – I loved the mentoring aspect particularly – and it kept me busy.

I was so excited to be in a big new city – there was so much to see and do, and the buzz and frenetic energy of Sydney was so different to Perth. I loved spending time in East Sydney, the queer capital of Australia, especially Darlinghurst and Surry Hills. There, being queer was completely normal – I'd never seen so many rainbow flags!

But I was not prepared for Sydney traffic. I had a work car so I could visit my clients, and sitting in gridlock made me feel so claustrophobic. I hated it. I found it so hard working out how to get around; Sydney felt like a maze that I would never understand. It might sound silly, but soon I was missing the familiar landmarks and places of home that I knew like the back of my hand – the Swan River, which I used as a guide to navigate my way around the city, the beach, my local supermarket and post office, my GP. It was difficult getting my head around the massive sprawl of Sydney — such a contrast to Perth, where you could drive for half an hour and be out in the bush, on country, or at any of the beaches, watching the sun sinking into the gold of the Indian Ocean at the end of a busy day. I loved the physical beauty of Sydney, and the beaches too, but getting around was so stressful sometimes!

Back home, my friends and community came from footy and being active, so when a colleague, Mel, suggested I come along to her gym and take part in a boxing class, I was super keen. I figured sport was likely to be how I'd make friends again, and I was right. Mel was a First Nations woman and we clicked immediately — to me, she felt like someone from home. At the gym she introduced me to another friend of hers, Vanessa, who was studying law with a focus on human rights and anti-discrimination law. We got along like a house on fire, too.

Soon I found a new place to live in Surry Hills and joined the social AFL 9s footy team at work. I loved how friendly people were in Surry Hills — there was always someone to chat to at the pub, or at Moore Park, where we played our footy games.

But no matter how hard I threw myself into creating a life in Sydney, the twinge of sadness I'd felt on the plane leaving Perth was ballooning into homesickness, and soon I was dogged by it. Every day, I woke up with dread in my stomach. I yearned for the familiar streets of Perth, but more importantly I felt so disconnected from country — the Noongar are water people, and the longer I was away from the regenerative power of the ocean and the beach, it really started to weigh on me. I didn't want to find myself cycling into another depressive episode.

I gave it a red hot go for about five or six months, and I know I was doing a good job at work. But you can only hide from the truth for so long, and eventually I just had to call it.

'I'm sorry,' I told Andrew at work. 'I love this job, and I want to thank you for giving me the opportunity, but I need to go home. I miss it too much.'

He was sorry to see me go, but as soon as I'd made the decision, it was as if the sun had come out. It was sad saying goodbye to Mel and Vanessa and my other new friends from footy, but I was aching to get back to my corner of the world.

I left as lightly as I had arrived, just me and two suitcases.

Even now I feel a little embarrassed that I didn't last longer in Sydney. There's part of me that feels that could have tried harder, that I wasn't tough enough, that I failed. But then I ask myself how I would have advised the young people I was working with if they were going through the same thing. I would have told them that giving something a go and deciding it isn't for them isn't failure. I would have told them that you have to pay attention to how you're feeling; that you have to trust your gut. There's no point in forcing something that feels wrong because you think you should, or because of other people's expectations. I'm glad I faced up to the way I was feeling and made a decision that put my emotional life first.

Besides, now I knew that sometimes things happen for a reason – and my life was about to change again in a big way.

Being back on Noongar country, I felt as if I could breathe again, and I needed to find a job and somewhere to live quickly. But at least I was home, and I felt immediately more grounded just for that fact.

While I was figuring out my next steps, I stayed with some friends, and spent time searching for a new job. Eventually I came across something that looked really interesting, a role at an Aboriginal corporation that supported Indigenous people living in remote communities in Western Australia, all in the furthest south-eastern reaches of the state on Ngaanyatjarra country, some bordering on the Northern Territory.

I became the only First Nations person working in the city office of about forty or fifty staff, which seemed remarkable to me for an organisation working directly with Indigenous clients – it was a bit of a shock having just come from AFL SportsReady, where my colleagues were mostly First Nations. My job was tenancy support for the communities, which would often be housing repairs or maintenance issues, and my role was to liaise with the people living there, log the issues and organise a tradesperson servicing those areas to fix them.

Because the communities were so remote it wasn't easy to keep things on track and make sure people got support when they needed it. From the get-go, I could see there were inefficiencies in the way the organisation responded to calls for assistance – it could sometimes take many weeks before an issue was resolved and I made it my mission to get as many issues worked out as I could, as quickly as possible, and began combining multiple repairs into one job or call-out with the tradies. My aim was to have issues fixed within a matter of days of being reported.

After a few weeks in my new job, I started looking for somewhere to live, and found a listing that looked promising, for an apartment close to the city with one other woman, Lulu.

When I turned up at the apartment to meet her, she answered the door with a glass of wine in her hand, and I knew we'd get along just fine! Lulu was so beautiful, a woman of colour from Zambia, and she had a really fun, outgoing personality, and worked as an accountant for a beauty school. We clicked immediately and became good friends, hanging out with glass of wine after work and watching TV together.

I also started playing footy again, for the Swan Districts this time, *and* rugby union, and I also discovered a passion for running. That year, I ran twelve kilometres in my first City to Surf, which was a goal I'd had for a while, and I was so stoked to tick it off. Later I would run a half-marathon, something I never thought I'd never do in my life. I'll never run a full marathon though – life is too short! I was so happy to be home and back in the swing of life in Perth again; I had my friends around me and could see my family. Life was good.

It was around this time that I was asked to take part in an interview with Noongar Dandjoo TV, a series about the issues affecting Noongar people – a collaboration between screen students at Curtin University and their Aboriginal Studies department and NITV (National Indigenous Television). They wanted to interview me at work as a young Noongar-Yamatji woman with a passion for supporting community, mental health awareness and footy. The film crew and producers came to interview me in the office and at home too, and we talked about my life growing up and the difficulties I'd had, and they invited Troy to be part of the interview as well. I'd taken part in a radio interview to promote Miss NAIDOC the year before, but this was the first television interview I'd ever done, and I felt instantly comfortable talking to the camera – maybe it was foreshadowing my TV career.

At work, occasionally I got the chance to travel out into the communities, which was a really eye-opening experience. Growing up in Carnarvon, I'd always felt as though I knew what it was like to live in an Aboriginal community – in a way I had, surrounded by other Noongar and Yamatji people, and we spent a lot of time on country, but we were still living in a conventional town with all the amenities you would expect. The remote places I visited weren't anything like I'd ever experienced. These were communities on remote desert country with only around 100 houses, with limited medical and educational services, and only one shop to supply basic needs. Because there was no other source for supplies and the distances in transporting them were huge, the prices for simple things like groceries were sky high.

The houses weren't fit for purpose either, or responsive to the cultural needs of the community. The plumbing and wiring or electrical supply was poor, and there would be instances of things being broken or ruined, not because people were reckless or malicious, but because they were trying to find a way to make what they had suit the cultural practices they were trying to follow.

For example, in one community, there weren't the amenities available to set up a fire outside so that a family could cook a roo tail, so they'd had to take the door off the oven in the house so they could fit it in – and it hadn't been fixed since. These things don't make sense to outsiders, but made perfect sense in community. Similarly, there would be issues when a person passed away in a house. That house then became a 'sorry house', and no one could enter it or use it. Sorry business is a serious and significant cultural practice and it has to be conducted properly, but that also meant that community had one less house available to people to live in. I could see that these communities didn't have the benefit of organisations working closely enough with them so that their needs were understood properly, and that in general, non-Indigenous people were making decisions on behalf of Indigenous folk.

People were so welcoming and kind to me when I visited those communities, but it was bittersweet. It was so rewarding to be around mob, to hear their stories and make real connections. Out there, away from the bustle of the city, I could feel country around me so strongly; and for those communities that sense of deep belonging is crucial to the way they live every day. But it was heartbreaking to see the way people were forced to live, with so little amenity and support. It was clear to me that, as Indigenous people, we have to make this awful choice between living remotely on country and being able to hold onto our culture but losing out on resources and support – or living like I had, growing up in bigger towns and cities with access to proper amenity and services, but which often came with a loss of culture.

These people could speak their language fluently. I had barely any language, just the few words of Noongar that Nan had passed on to me. But I'd always had access to school, to healthcare, to sport, because of where I lived. It shouldn't be this either-or scenario, though. I kept wondering, surely there's a way to make it easier for people to live remotely. If we can build roads, why can't we build better infrastructure? Why can't we create a supply chain for better access to basic resources? Why can't we work with the community to find a way to honour sorry business and still keep houses habitable? It seemed to me that what we were doing in our work was just putting Band-Aids on much bigger, systemic problems because they were too hard and complex to fix.

All of these thoughts gnawed at me, and in an effort to do my best, the more efficient I became in my role, the more duties were added to my position description, and soon I felt overloaded with work. It also seemed to me that my First Nations heritage was being used to gloss over cultural issues in the organisation – I was asked to do Acknowledgements of Country for events and meetings, and meanwhile I was one of the lowest paid members of the team.

The last straw for me came when I broke my collarbone playing rugby. I had to get it set, and I remember being at work with the injury still fresh, and being told we were about to begin a big audit process, which I was expected to complete on top of all my regular duties. I was in pain, I was frustrated with the workload, and I could see that the systems weren't going to change. I resigned.

When I arrived home that day, caught between pride for backing myself, and worry at the prospect of yet again not having a job, Lulu toasted my courage with a glass of wine, and I did what had worked for me in the past – I put the word out on Facebook to say that I was looking for work.

Not long after I'd posted, a friend, Naomi, sent me a direct message.

'Hi Brooke, have you worked with Aboriginal kids?' she asked.

'Yes, I have, and I have a diploma in Youth Work,' I typed back quickly.

'I think I have something for you!'

Naomi put me in touch with the manager of youth services at the City of Gosnells council. He was looking for a casual youth worker to run programs like drop-in services and after-school programs for young people in the south of Perth. There was a fairly high population of Indigenous kids in the area, so I'd get to work with mob and focus on engaging kids with school, and helping them with their attendance and their homework, and generally boost their skills and confidence. It sounded a lot like Follow the Dream, which had helped me so much at school, and I leapt at the opportunity.

I loved everything about that job. I got to design and organise programs from start to finish, hang out with young people, build rapport and then help them when and where they needed it. In a way, I felt as if I was paying my own good luck forward, because it was so much like the help that Jo had given me when I was a lost and troubled teen.

Connecting with the kids I was working with came so naturally to me. My office had an open-door policy, and I made sure that if anyone wanted to see me, they always felt welcome. I kept a big jar of chocolates on my desk, which was a good way of getting kids in the door and breaking the ice. Once we got chatting, I could find out more about their circumstances and start thinking of ways of supporting them to stay engaged at school.

I dealt with some pretty confronting cases, even for someone like me who'd grown up with a lot of trauma and poverty. I remember there was one girl, only fourteen years old, who was working as a prostitute to support herself. Her family either didn't know or didn't care, and she was so disengaged, it was really hard to connect with her at first. I hoped that with simple perseverance, like taking her out for coffee every week, I'd be able to find some connection, and I did, and over time I managed to find out a bit more about her circumstances and was able to connect her up with some more support services.

It was a big job, but I knew what I was doing was important and had tangible, valuable outcomes for young people, and that meant a lot to me.

One evening, I came home from the gym to find Lulu tapping away at her laptop on the couch. ·

'What are you up to?' I asked, curious.

'I'm applying to go on *The Bachelor*,' she said, grinning at me. 'Did you know they've never had a woman of colour as a contestant?'

'That's crazy,' I said, coming over to look over her shoulder. Sure enough, there was an application form open on her screen for the sixth season of the show, and she had filled out most of it. 'Wow, would you really do it?'

'Hell, yeah, I would,' she said, laughing. 'Maybe I'll meet the man of my dreams! You should apply too. They've never had an Aboriginal contestant either.'

'Yeah, sure,' I joked, 'They'd be lucky to have me.'

I'd watched some episodes of *The Bachelor* living with Ronnie and Teneille, and more recently with Lulu, but I'd never seen an entire season. I thought it was funny watching twenty girls jerpin' for one man! But the next day at work, I found myself googling the application process and giving it a skim. It looked like a lot of fun, and I'd really enjoyed the television interview I'd done with Noongar Dandjoo TV. And there was something about what Lulu had said that had stuck in my head.

Why not throw my hat into the ring? Maybe I should do it, if only to see whether an Aboriginal girl like me could make it onto mainstream television.

It's fair to say I was utterly shocked when I got a phone call a few days later inviting me to a group audition with casting agents at a hotel in the city. Lulu wished me luck and said that it was just as well she wasn't coming – she reckoned she was far too opinionated to be on telly! I had no idea what a group audition would entail, but I figured I'd come this far so I should definitely give it a go.

I arrived at the audition with about a hundred other girls, expecting to be asked a few questions and do some role play. I wasn't too far off the mark, but it was definitely more intense than I'd expected. Anyone who's had experience of the performing arts will have a good idea of the kind of thing the scouts wanted to know: what we were like as people, how willing and comfortable we'd be to try new things and throw ourselves into the experience, and I guess they also wanted to see the chemistry between us as potential contestants, how we'd interact.

That afternoon is still a blur to me. The group audition process took hours, and I rocketed between feeling really confident and feeling completely out of my depth. At the end of the day the shortlist from the group audition was announced, and somehow I'd made it into the final six.

Then we took part in another round of interviews, this time under the hot, bright glare of proper television lighting, and it wasn't until then that the reality of what I was doing – putting myself forward as a potential contestant of *The Bachelor* – hit home. One of the requirements of being confirmed in the shortlist was whether we were single and genuinely looking for a relationship – and that was another moment when the reality of what I was doing struck me. Since Sally and I had broken up, I'd been on my own for a while, and I was ready to find someone special again. It all felt so surreal.

After the audition, I went back to my normal life and work, expecting that to be the end of it. But to my complete shock, only a few weeks later I received a call from the producers telling me I'd been selected as one of the twenty-two contestants for the show.

Suddenly I had a huge decision to make. There aren't many scenarios in life where you need to take the equivalent of three months off work and sever contact with everyone you know. But remembering Jo's sage advice about taking risks, I took a deep breath ... and said yes.

After swearing them to secrecy under pain of death, I told my brothers as well as a few close friends about what I was doing, then let work know that I needed to take time off, and was assured they'd have work for me if or when I needed it later. Then I paid my rent in advance with Lulu, and packed up my things to travel back to Sydney, where filming would take place at an undisclosed location, and where I'd have no contact with the outside world. Later, I'd discover that Leanne had become really worried about me when she couldn't track me down, and Troy reassured her that I hadn't gone missing, and that I was alive and well!

I've made a deliberate decision not to go into a lot of detail about competing in my seasons of *The Bachelor* and *Bachelor in Paradise*. The shows are available to watch, or re-watch, and there's an ocean of opinion about what happened on each one. Viewers draw their own conclusions, and as a participant you have to be OK with that, which I was, and I still am. Going into filming for each of the programs I made a decision to just enjoy the process as much as I could and just be myself.

What I will say is that nothing prepares you for the production process. When we'd wrapped on the first gruelling day on set,

I could see that a lot of the contestants, myself included, were feeling shell-shocked. Perhaps it was the youth worker in me, but I knew that the best remedy for the situation was for us to understand that we were all in it together, and I gathered everyone out on the lounge on the outdoor patio of the house. Then, one by one, we shared with each other how we how we were feeling. One of the girls had brought a set of bongo drums with her to the house, and another had brought a guitar, and soon we were having a singalong and a laugh, and it really helped to break the ice. I think we all needed it, and it was great to feel a warm sense of community and shared experience.

I certainly never expected to be one of the final three contestants of *The Bachelor*, and I also didn't expect the strength of the genuine feelings I had for Nick Cummins. When I made my decision to leave the show before Nick chose whether I would be in the final two, it was because I was starting to feel my confidence and my mental health slipping, and I needed to take back some control.

I was really glad that I left the show on my own terms, and I still am. I had true feelings for Nick, and I needed to protect myself. I don't think anyone knows what they're in for when they go on a reality dating program until they're there – you might think that you're ready for the intensity and the highs and lows of filming, and that you won't get too emotionally invested, but when you meet someone and spend time with them like you do on the *Bachelor* programs, all bets are off. I left the show feeling sad and heartbroken, and headed back home to Perth and to the safety and love of my friends and family.

Filming for the program finished in June in 2018, and I couldn't disclose what happened in the season until it had finished airing. The season would start its run on Network Ten in October, so until then I tried to put it all out of my mind by throwing myself back into my youth work and staying fit. Then out of the blue, Jeremy Bruce, my old football coach from high school, got in touch with me about a potential job.

Meeting up for coffee was a blast from the past. There's no surer sign of having grown up than meeting with an old teacher and realising that you're peers. Jeremy was just as gruff and friendly as he had been all that time ago at school, and thanks to his connections with mutual friends, he'd been watching my career in youth work flourish over the years.

'I've got a role for you if you want it,' he told me. 'It's a big one, but I reckon you'd be perfect for it.'

Jeremy was operating a full-service school program for all the high schools in the Armadale area, a Western Australian government initiative supporting at-risk students who were transitioning out of school and needed help staying engaged with an educational program or working through their next steps. The service was run out of a hub on the Armadale Senior High School premises, and while it was an intense job, it was the perfect fit for me.

I would spend days looking at lists of students who had been absent from school, and more days doing detective work figuring out where they were. Then I'd spend my time tracking them down so I could chat to them, entice them to come to a program, and hopefully build enough trust and rapport to connect them to an educational service or a traineeship.

I loved it, and it kept me so busy that *The Bachelor* faded into the background. Later, I'd work in other government programs in the same kind of role, and in a heartbreaking twist, the car

I drove on my expeditions to track down the kids I wanted to engage with had blue government plates – the same kind of blue plates that I remembered Mum telling us about. The same kind of blue plates that meant we should hide whenever we saw them coming.

And there I was, driving the car. With the memories of the fear I felt seeing those blue plates on a car pulling up outside our house, I always made sure to park as far away as I could, or was practical, when I was making a home visit.

My work with these kids made me think a lot about what could have gone differently for us all if we'd had the right intervention at the right time. If Mum had been supported more, would she have avoided the addiction that took over her life, would she have received help for her mental health? Would Ky have been encouraged to stay at school with her own cycles of addiction and mental ill-health interrupted? Perhaps as siblings we could all have grown up together, instead of being separated at such young ages.

Every time I met a new child or youth, I saw an opportunity to help turn their lives around, to help them avoid falling through the cracks the way Mum had, the way Ky had. It didn't always work, of course, and for every hundred or so kids who were identified as 'at-risk' in my investigations, I would end up working with only around thirty.

It's not like the movies, where the bright-eyed, principled young social worker arrives in a rough neighbourhood and with a few big grand gestures, magically changes lives for the better. The reality is that it's often the simple, small things that are the most effective – like putting on a feed after school, and helping kids with their homework, just like Follow the Dream did for me.

Eventually I was running a girls group, and I'd organise beauty days where we'd make face masks, or baking days, cooking cakes or even pies, just like Barb, my foster carer, had with me. The goal was simply to provide positive experiences and build confidence in the kids in my care so they'd open up about their life and their challenges – and then find the most effective ways of supporting them.

It was the most fulfilling work I've ever done, and soon it would bring my journey to a full circle.

While Jo had moved on from Follow the Dream at Cecil Andrews College – she'd returned to primary school teaching – the woman who was now managing the program had heard that I was working in youth education, and she invited me to come and work there too. I was thrilled, and agreed immediately, and when I first arrived back on campus, it was such a strange experience – here I was, walking back onto the grounds of my old school as a twenty-three-year-old woman: confident, committed and professional, and there to make a difference. The contrast between who I was now and the scared, troubled little girl I'd been at the beginning of high school was sharp – and made even sharper when I walked around to the teachers' lounge and saw my name on the plaque of Head Girls outside.

Soon though, *The Bachelor* would start making a real impact on my life. The series screening dates on Network Ten had been announced and the first few news stories were beginning to be published in the traditional and social media.

Oh God, here it comes, I thought.

Once filming had ended, some of us from the show had stayed in touch with each other (and have remained friends to this day), but in truth we were all very keen to get back to our normal lives, and I'd been so busy with work and staying fit I'd been able to push it out of my mind most of the time. I wasn't ready to see it all unfold on TV, so when the first episode was going to air, I was relieved when one of my oldest friends, Tess, invited me to watch it at her place so she could give me the moral support I needed.

I was anxious as hell. I had no idea how I would come across, and watching myself on screen, baring my soul and my interest in Nick to the world was very confronting. Just as shocking was my phone blowing up with messages of support, and at every ad break, watching the followers on my Instagram account grow by the thousands. At the end of the first episode, more than 30,000 people had started following me, and I'd received hundreds of messages of support – people telling me how much they admired me, how much they loved my energy, and that they were excited to see what I'd do in the next episode.

It was the first time I'd ever heard of the term 'front runner' – apparently, I was one, according to my newly found fans. As for the people I knew, I reckon I heard from everyone I'd ever met in my life that night! Mob were sharing the episode on their socials and celebrating the fact that there was an Aboriginal girl on telly, and later my footy mates would be cheering about seeing my queer relationship history acknowledged on TV screens around the country.

The rest of the season airing was just as intense, and throughout I felt a bit like a time traveller, knowing what was coming on the show and how things would unfold episode to episode.

It wasn't much later that I was asked to take part in *Bachelor in Paradise*. This time I really had to think about it before I said yes. My gut was saying no – the attention I was receiving was overwhelming sometimes, but I also wanted to know if there was a new path for me professionally, too. I loved my youth work – it was my passion – but there were contestants who'd already agreed to be on *Paradise* who I was keen to meet. I also couldn't deny the fact that the income I'd be earning would be very helpful; it meant that I could help support my family more, and in fact, that year I was able to afford to host Christmas in Perth, which my brothers attended.

In the end, *Bachelor in Paradise* was much less of a positive experience for me – after the intensity of filming *The Bachelor*, I wasn't emotionally ready to be back in front of the cameras so soon, and I felt that the edit of the show didn't necessarily tell the whole story. Sharing the first same-sex kiss with Alex Nation on reality television in Australia was a pretty big milestone, and I felt proud to normalise queer attraction and love, but I do think it could have been handled differently and more respectfully by the show. Again, I left the show heartbroken.

Paradise wouldn't air for a few months after we'd filmed, but within a year both seasons were well and truly behind me, and I fell into a new normal, working for the government-backed youth service and juggling the requests I was beginning to receive as someone in the public eye.

It's not an easy transition from living a 'normal' life to having an audience of hundreds of thousands. Truth be told, my 'normal' wasn't normal at all – only two years before, I'd been on the brink of another mental health crisis and had always had to think carefully about my next steps to keep a roof over my head. Now I was someone that so many Australians considered an 'influencer'. It felt so strange, but it was also exciting to see such a supportive community open up to me, a young queer, Aboriginal woman from a tough background.

I had no formal training in social media or marketing, so did what came naturally and simply started treating my Instagram account as an extension of me. To be honest, I think the same thing drew people to me at school, work, and footy and my other circles of friends was what drew people to me online: I was just myself. I didn't know how to be anything else, and for my entire life I've never held back from saying what I think.

From that moment onwards, I shared my thoughts and feelings about the things I was interested in, about the things and people who inspire me, and my community just grew and grew. To this day, I know that my audience loves me, and I love them, though the term 'influencer' doesn't sit comfortably with me – I prefer to think of myself more as a First Nations content creator, or Indigenous creative. But like anyone with a public profile, I get trolls and messages of hate, and part of that is because I get held to standards that straight white women don't. But I've learned to take the good with the ugly … and generally ignore the ugly!

In the beginning, though, it was a lot for me to take on board and I was aching for some stability in the whirlwind of my busy life of my day-to-day job, and media calls, invitations to events, creative collaborations, and requests for sponsorship partnerships.

Very soon I found that stability, but not in the form I was expecting.

I'd been invited to a fancy polo match in the city – it was sponsored by a luxury car brand, and it was the first time I'd ever received a free ticket to an event like this. A friend suggested we go together, and truth be told I was curious to see what it would be like, especially if there were horses involved. Ever since working with Buddy and Ray in those early mornings with Jo, horses would always hold a special place in my heart. The polo match would be the poshest thing I'd ever been to, and I figured it would be a bit of a laugh – and I never could resist getting dolled up.

As well as the main event – a match played by some of Perth's most elite polo players – there were all kinds of other silly games for spectators, including a 'ladies race', which saw women dressed to absolute nines racing against each other on foot. Never one to resist a competitive sprint, I kicked my heels off and lined up.

When the starting gun went off, I went for it, and I was neck and neck with another young woman when she practically threw herself at the finish line, knocking me over in the process. I took the tumble as gracefully as I could, and was laughing breathlessly as I got up to shake the hand of the winner.

And then, as I turned away towards the stands, there he was, a vaguely familiar figure standing off to one side. Within a moment I'd placed him, and as he came forward, I smiled.

'Hey Brooke,' he said with a shy grin. 'I don't know if you remember me. I'm Nick.'

'Yeah, I remember you,' I said, grinning back. 'Surprised you remember me, though!'

Nick was a helicopter pilot who I'd met at the mining company, when I was working on reception. I was used to saying hello to all the hotshots who came into head office, especially him – perhaps because I thought he was handsome; perhaps because I thought there'd always been a little spark of interest between us.

I slipped my heels back on and we started chatting, and the attraction was instantaneous, as sudden as if fate had brought us together.

Soon we'd fallen head over heels for each other. Nick and I were spending every waking moment together, but we lived on different sides of town, so it made sense for me to move in with him. At the time, Nick was working on his own new start-up business in the mining industry, and flying helicopters was something he did on the weekends. My job with the youth work program had finished up and I started working more for myself, splitting my time between consulting and doing contract work for mental health and youth programs, and doing more work as an Indigenous creative with the requests that were coming my way.

Nick was a such a loving, supportive partner, and it was the strongest, most secure relationship I'd had in my entire life. While I'd always remember where I'd come from, for the whole time we were together, it almost seemed possible to forget about the troubles of my past, and I leant into a new, empowered version of myself.

Of course, to all of my new followers online and the people I was meeting in real life, they saw a polished, put-together version of me. They saw the woman I'd become, but they had little insight into how much I'd had to overcome to get there – the trauma of my childhood, and the poverty I grew up with, which will always be a part of who I am. It was hard sometimes, trying to reconcile the glitz and glamour of a creative gig, and knowing that some members of my extended family were struggling. That I had relatives who were caught in cycles of addiction and poverty. That my siblings and I were separated, and I wasn't always sure how they were doing.

Ky was the hardest to stay connected to. Unlike Troy, Eden and RJ, who I was able to maintain contact with via text or social media, Ky had no phone and no fixed address.

As far as I knew then, Ky was back in Carnarvon, but it was hard to know for certain. She'd been in and out of mental health facilities like Graylands in Perth, and she'd also been in and out of prison on minor charges. I knew she was most likely to be using drugs.

If there was something I'd learned in all of my twenty-three years, it was that even if you want to avoid your past, it'll always come and find you. My worlds were due to collide, and they did in a spectacular way one day, when I was walking down a busy city street with Nick, out shopping for the day.

Somehow, out of nowhere, there was Ky.

She walked straight past me, and I stopped still in my tracks. I turned and jogged to catch up with her, reaching out to touch her on the shoulder.

'Ky?' It was definitely her.

She was just skin and bones. Her hair was straggly, and she smelled terrible; her clothes were old and dirty, just tracksuit pants and a jumper. She looked out of it.

'Hey sis, it's you,' she said in her slow, gentle voice. She was smiling, but I felt like crying.

Struggling as I was in that moment to see the state my sister was in, there was another part of me that was hyper aware of Nick, who was now standing beside me. While Nick knew everything about me and my family, seeing the reality of Ky's circumstances would have been shocking for him. I hate to admit it, but there was part of me that was ashamed. I didn't want him to know what that reality looked like. I didn't want him to think that reality could be a part of mine.

But I should have known better. Nick was a good soul, with a massive heart, and he loved me unconditionally. He introduced himself to Ky, and he didn't think twice about putting our plans for the day aside so I could help my sister.

'Where are you living right now?' I asked Ky, moving her out of the way of the foot traffic so we could talk.

'In this hostel, hey,' she said, looking around. It was hard to get her to focus, but that was one of the symptoms of the schizophrenia she'd suffered from for most of her adult life.

I took her to a convenience store nearby and bought some food for her. I tried to pick things that didn't need a fridge and were easy to prepare, like two-minute noodles, canned soup and bread.

At the checkout, Ky nudged me. 'Can ya get me some smokes too?'

I wouldn't support her drug use, but given how little else she had, I wasn't going to deny her cigarettes. I asked the cashier to add a packet to the groceries.

As Nick and I followed Ky to her hostel, I tried to find out more from her about how she was, where she was spending her days. I wasn't getting very far, though.

The hostel she was staying in was really dingy, a true house of horrors. The people who were coming and going ranged along the full spectrum of hardship, addiction and mental illness. Not even the woman on the reception desk looked particularly well; she looked at me vacantly and then turned away, shrugging, when I asked her how long Ky had been staying there.

'Where's your room?' I asked Ky, trying not to let my dismay show on my face.

'Just here, sis,' she said, ambling slowly past the woman on the desk, to the first door in the corridor. She pushed the door open – it was unlocked, and so close to the entrance. I couldn't help but worry immediately how safe she was in this place.

'And this is *your* room? I mean, it's paid for?' I asked, as we followed her inside.

She shrugged.

If I thought Ky looked rough, that was nothing compared to the state of her room. It was small, with a single bed and a table. The whole room reeked of urine, and there was rubbish and used needles on the floor. There were no sheets or blankets on her bed, there was no window to let in air. It was horrific.

'Just give me a second,' I said to Nick. 'Can you wait outside in the street?' He nodded and squeezed my arm, then respectfully walked out so I could focus on Ky.

I put the food I'd bought for her on the table, and used the plastic carry bag to pick up some rubbish on the floor. It was the least I could do for the moment – I would come back the next day and help some more.

'Just wait here for a sec, OK, Ky?' I said, and headed back to the reception desk.

'Excuse me?' I asked the woman at the desk. 'Can you tell me who's paying for the room my sister's in?'

'What?' the receptionist asked, looking confused.

'Who booked that room?' I said, pointing at the door to Ky's room. 'Do you know who paid for it?'

It took a while, but finally she was able to tell me the Office of the Public Trustee for Western Australia had organised for her to stay there. I googled their number and then spent half an hour on the phone, pacing around the hostel foyer confirming that Ky's room was indeed reserved for her, and that it was being paid for by that government agency.

At least she has a roof over her head, I thought.

Ky was lying down and half asleep when I told her that I'd be back the next day. When I met Nick outside, he didn't ask many questions and we were both quiet, consumed by our own thoughts on the way back home.

If my sense of dissonance was strong leaving Ky in her piss-soaked hostel room, returning to our nice, neat, clean suburban house with every mod con sent it sky-rocketing. That night I could barely sleep, tormented at the thought of Ky huddled on her stinking mattress.

The next day, I left the house early, and headed to Target. I bought a set of sheets, a doona and a doona cover, a pillow and some towels. Then I went to the supermarket and bought toiletries, and a bucket, a mop and cleaning supplies.

At the hostel, Ky was nowhere to be seen, but as expected, her door wasn't locked so I set to work cleaning. I picked up the rubbish from the floor, taking care with the used needles, and stuffed her stuffed her dirty clothes into a garbage bag to take home with me to wash. Everything smelled so bad. I filled the bucket in the communal bathroom and mopped the floor of her room, and I cleaned and wiped every surface. I lay the toiletries out for Ky on the table next to her bed, made the bed with the sheets and the doona, and left the new towels folded on her fresh pillow.

Before I'd left home, I'd tucked a few photographs of our family into my handbag – of Mum, Nan, Eden, Troy, me and RJ. Now, I pulled them out and tacked them to the wall next to her bed. Surveying the room, I took a deep breath – hopefully a clean and neat environment would do something for the state of Ky's mental health. Perhaps she'd be there when I brought her clean clothes back for her the next day and I'd be able to find out more about her life, and what more I could do.

When I got home, I put her clothes in the washing machine and stared aimlessly as they spun around and around, still reeling with the shock of what I'd seen the last twenty-four hours. How could Ky be living in squalor and danger when I was living a life of comfort and security?

I started thinking about what I could do to help her. Should I rent a house for her, so she had somewhere safe and clean to live? But I'd seen the state of her room at the hostel. What would I do if she trashed it, or if she let other damaged people move in with her? I wasn't even sure if I could afford to rent accommodation for her in the long term. So much of me was aching to leap into action and try and put her life right, but I also remembered how this story usually ended. I'd seen Mum and Ky go through enough cycles of addiction and ill health to know that I couldn't actually save her.

The next day, I went back with Ky's clean clothes. When I opened the door, I could have wept. It was as if I'd never been there – everything I'd cleaned so painstakingly with my mop and all my childish optimism looked to have been returned to its previous state. The room reeked of piss again, and the sheets had been torn from the bed, the table overturned.

Ky's sleeping form was under the doona, and when I got closer, I could see blood running down the side of her face. She'd clearly hurt herself. Angrily I brushed away the tears that were now making their way down my cheeks, and shook her awake.

'What have you done to yourself?' I muttered, as she gradually came to. 'Come on sis, let's get you cleaned up.'

I gathered a towel and the toiletries from the floor of her room and led her to the communal bathroom, where I helped her get her clothes off and into the shower. Gently I washed the blood away from the graze on her forehead, then helped her shampoo and condition her hair. I patted her dry with a towel and helped her dress in the clean clothes I'd brought back for her. Then we went back to her dirty room and I put her back to bed.

For a moment, I stood and watched Ky. Soon she was asleep again, like an island rooted firmly amid the chaos.

I had to accept that I wasn't my sister's keeper. I couldn't fix Ky's life, or make her better. I didn't have the skills or the resources to help her overcome her addiction, to help her manage her mental health. I wanted to, more than anything, but I was still figuring out my own life. I didn't know how to figure hers out too. I didn't know what would help make a difference in her life while she was in this state. I knew that even if I continued to try to fix things, like I had the day before, she'd simply destroy it all over again, and we'd be caught in an endless cycle of hopelessness.

I wrote down my phone number and left it on her table. I left it with the woman at the reception desk too, so she could call me if anything happened.

I didn't hear from Ky, or see her again, for a while after that.

Nine

For a brief period, life took on an easy rhythm. With *The Bachelor* behind me, and the support of a loving, stable relationship, I started to really hustle in my career. Soon I was working with lots of different organisations, advising and consulting on youth work programs, with a finer focus on suicide prevention in First Nations communities.

Occasionally when I'd walk into a meeting room full of old white men the energy in the room sometimes felt hostile, as if they were thinking, 'What can this little black girl teach me?' But by then I'd grown in confidence, and I knew what I was offering was important and could help save lives, so I just looked them in the eye and didn't waver in my advice or suggestions. I think I earned real respect.

Some really exciting opportunities came my way at this stage. One of the best was being asked by the University of Western Australia to give a TEDx talk about my experiences growing up, and I said yes, immediately – to me that request came at exactly the right time.

I loved having such a big, engaged audience, but it was struggle sometimes to see how some people – fans, the media, even strangers on the street – saw me in a particular way, and put me in a box: the girl from *The Bachelor* with a glamorous, easy life. While I hadn't broadcast the details of my family life and the trauma and hardship I'd suffered growing up, I'd never hidden the toughness of my background as an Aboriginal person, or shied away from talking about or expressing my queerness, and the assumptions about who I was bothered me. One of the other things that bothered me was that some people saw me as a damsel in distress who needed to be 'saved' by Nick on *The Bachelor*, and that wasn't true either.

Those assumptions meant that a lot of people didn't see the real me, and I wanted to make sure everyone could, especially any young girl or woman who was living with poverty and disadvantage in their lives. I knew how important visibility is in breaking down stereotypes, and now I had an opportunity to talk about my story with more nuance than just headlines in entertainment news items and snapshots and soundbites on my Instagram account.

I worked with some incredible women from the TEDx unit at the university, who coached me over the weeks leading up to the event and helped me write my presentation. With those girls and young women living with disadvantage firmly in mind, I talked about my life, how I'd had to negotiate labels all my life, how I firmly believe that it is possible to transcend the worst that life can throw at you. I made sure to talk about the real details – some of the darkest of my life – and hoped they'd connect with any young person watching, to show them that they could change their own stories, their own narratives.

It was one of the most gratifying things I ever did, and I still get goosebumps whenever I watch it. I can see that the young woman on stage is still working out who she is, but there's a wily strength there too.

But just as one part of my life was really taking off, another chapter was coming to an end. After almost two years together, and having built a beautiful life with each other, Nick and I broke up. There was a ten-year age gap between us, and the longer we were together, the more that gap made itself felt. We were just at different stages in our life. We were both heartbroken, but we knew we needed to make the decision to quit while we were ahead, to save us any more heartbreak later.

It was around Christmas when we broke up, and RJ had just been visiting in Perth. Eden and his partner, Jacqui, now had a baby boy, Tyrell, and they hadn't been able to make it down from Karratha for Christmas.

I really wanted to spend some time on my own, and I needed a reason to hit the road. So I offered to drive RJ back to Carnarvon, with the plan of driving further north to Karratha to see Eden and Jacqui, and give Tyrell his Christmas present. After that, all I wanted to do was drive on by myself and see where the road took me. I needed to get out of the city, to be alone on country. There's something so liberating about the highway stretching out ahead of you and nothing holding you back. It frees the soul.

The drive to Carnarvon with RJ was beautiful – spending one-on-one time with my little brother and getting to know him as the young adult he was at the time was so precious to me.

I'd been back to Carnarvon regularly over the years for RJ's birthday, and it still felt like home; I think it always will. It was bittersweet driving through the familiar streets and landmarks from my childhood. Memories of Nan and Mum were everywhere, and it wouldn't have surprised me in the least if I'd seen the old silver Commodore cruising around a corner with Mum at the wheel, one arm hanging out the window.

Catching up with mob was enlivening – it felt as if there was a part of me that had been suppressed and now it was making its way back out. It was then that I understood how much I'd been pushing the old Brooke down around people who didn't know my past. Ever since I'd arrived in Perth, I'd been editing myself to fit the expectations of people around me, even more so since appearing on *The Bachelor* and *Bachelor in Paradise*. It was taking a toll on me, and being with mob, and being back on country, released a pressure valve in me I didn't know I had.

Soon I was on my way to Karratha, where I spent some wonderful days with Eden, Jacqui and Tyrell. When my car pulled into their driveway, and Tyrell – only a tiny toddler – came rushing out to meet me, I felt my heart fill up. I'd needed this, I needed my family. Holding his little body close filled me with joy.

After my visit, the road was calling me further north, and drove all the way to Broome. I packed extra food and water, in case I ran into any trouble, but it felt good to be alone, just me and my own thoughts in the car. The country around me was stunning – red desert sand, the sky vast and blue overhead.

In Broome, I checked into a little Airbnb and made myself comfortable, and then suddenly it was just me and the silence. Seeing my family had been a balm, but there was no escape now from working through what I was feeling – how afraid I was in losing Nick, how uncomfortable I felt when I was alone, how much I looked to relationships to fill me up.

This might sound corny, but there in that Airbnb, I found some really great TEDx talks, videos and articles by women who inspired me to think differently about my life, who could show me the benefits of being on my own, and being OK about it. One woman in particular, Lane Moore, a former sex and relationships editor at US *Cosmopolitan*, really inspired me; it was almost as if her book *How to be Alone, If You Want To, and Even If You Don't* was written for me and me alone. How could I ever find a meaningful relationship if I didn't first have one with myself?

Later that night, I got dressed and steeled myself for one experience I always avoided: eating in public on my own. It made me feel so self-conscious – it still does! – as if I'm expecting people to judge me at every turn. Then I overthink it, and I can't relax. But that night, I was determined to get over it. I screwed all my courage together, googled a good place to eat nearby and made my way there.

It was a busy pub, and once I'd found myself a quiet place at the end of the bar to sit down, I ordered my meal and tried to ignore the urge to look at my phone. I forced myself just sit there with my thoughts, and deal with the fact I was on my own.

'Hi,' someone said behind me.

I turned around to see a young woman who was smiling at me. 'I just noticed you're here by yourself,' she said. 'Would you like to come and eat with us?'

She gestured at a table close by, where there were a couple of guys, who waved.

'Oh wow, thanks,' I said, a little flustered. 'Yeah, that would be great!'

That night I made friendships that have stayed with me ever since. I realised that if I'd been with Nick (or with anyone else I was in a romantic relationship with), I would never have had the opportunity to meet those new people, because no one would have interrupted our night out. Being in a relationship can be amazing, but I was just beginning to understand that being single had its own benefits too – including the fact that it would open me up to all kinds of new people and experiences.

When I left Broome a few days later, my cup was a little more full. I took the drive home to Perth slowly, stopping when I needed to between long stretches behind the wheel.

There was one last place I wanted to visit before I went back to my busy life.

I wanted to commune with Mum and Nan, and there was only one place for that – the Quobba blowholes and beach. Driving into the park, I stopped at the ranger's station to get my permit.

'You here alone?' the ranger asked, glancing through the window of my car.

'Oh, my boyfriend is coming later today to join me,' I lied, suddenly realising how vulnerable I was – a woman on her own, heading into isolated bush to camp overnight. It was pretty flimsy protection, but it quelled any unease I felt.

I drove to the clifftops where we used to camp with Mum when we were kids. Just being there, I felt closer to her. I pulled out the tent, set up my camp, and then walked to the best spot along the cliffs where you can gaze down at the blowholes and the ocean stretches out in front of you, as far as the eye can see. It was beautiful, and watching the spray from the blowholes glint in the red sun as it started its slide into the horizon, the ocean scent all around me, the soft breeze on my skin, all I felt was peace. Then I walked the short distance to the white sands of the beach and as I swam in the water, it felt as if the ocean was washing away all the pain of the breakup with Nick. I felt strong. I felt more like myself than I had in a long time.

Country always grounds me, and water is so central to who I am, who my people are. There on the beach it felt as if Mum and Nan could hear every thought, that they were there with me, taking in the sorrow I felt, and reflecting back the strength and hope I knew I had inside me too.

I slept that night better than I had in months. I spent the drive back to Perth thinking about what I wanted to do next. I knew I'd be mourning the end of my relationship with Nick for some time, but I wanted to put some plans in place for my future. This trip had been so restorative, and I knew I needed to put romantic love to one side for a while and focus on my goals. I knew I had the skills to continue working for myself, and I had the passion to make an impact in my area of expertise. I also wanted to give university another shot.

When I arrived back home in Perth, I applied to study for a Diploma in Psychology at Curtin University, and set my intention to start a new chapter of my life.

Then the pandemic arrived on our shores.

There are many things I'm grateful for in the crazy life I've led, but one of the biggest in recent years is that I escaped poverty before COVID-19 hit in 2020. When I think about the way my family lived when I was growing up, and how contagious and deadly the disease is, I know we would have been decimated.

Because our immunity is already so low across the board, First Nations people have an extremely high risk of death or long-term symptoms from COVID-19, and there was a huge, coordinated effort from mob to work hard to keep rural and remote communities around the country safe. In those areas particularly, poverty – and the domestic overcrowding and lower capacity for hygiene that comes hand-in-hand with that – and reduced access to quality health services increase the chances of infectious diseases like COVID of having a far worse impact than on the general population.

If my family had still been living in Carnarvon the way we were when I was growing up, with people coming in and out of our house, us kids sharing a bed with Nan, and no real focus on hygiene, or even nutrition, we would have caught the virus, and fast. And Nan, and my aunties and uncles, who all had their own complex health conditions from a lifetime of disadvantage and poverty, would most likely have died sooner than was than fair.

As it is, too many people from every walk of life suffered with the effects and restrictions of the pandemic, and in a way it was a strangely uniting experience; a bit of an equaliser. But I'm very conscious that my experience in lockdown and with the virus in general wasn't the worst – I was studying, I was still getting work, and even though restrictions meant I couldn't get out to the organisations I was working with, or socialise, I knew I'd be OK.

That year was certainly a shake-up, as it was for everyone, and I managed to get through it with the help of new friends and a new home. When Nick and I broke up, I bounced around a few different share-houses, and eventually moved in with a friend, Alex, who felt a little like a younger brother to me.

That year also marked the arrival of a very special character in my life – a tiny little hound called Cobar. I've always loved animals, and in those first few months of the pandemic, I was yearning for a dog in my life. Growing up in Carnarvon, there were always dogs around at home, but poverty doesn't create the best environment for looking after them properly.

After a bit of research, I found my puppy – a tiny little King Charles Cavalier, cocker spaniel and poodle cross, who I named Cobar. His arrival was such a source of joy during lockdown for me and Alex, and he's been the light of my life ever since.

I was also starting to realise my dream of working in suicide prevention for Aboriginal and Torres Strait Islander people. I'd started making some great contacts and delivering one-off and longer-term mental health programs with young people, and then I started being invited to work in prison environments, bringing cultural programs to women who were in the system.

It was so rewarding to be helping women in those circumstances – I could see how only a little support and empowerment could go a long way. We used trust-building exercises used commonly in theatre to help build confidence and connect the women with each other and with their goals for when they were released.

It was bittersweet for me, though, because my own sister had just left one of the prisons I was working at. Since I'd seen Ky at her hostel in Perth, she'd fallen pregnant with her second baby and had landed in prison on assault charges. I'd been to see her once or twice, and had been surprised by how well she was doing – in prison, Ky took her medication, wasn't drinking or taking drugs, and was determined to take care of the baby was carrying. But I'd seen this before with Ky, when she was pregnant with her first baby, Bubba Shane, and I knew what was coming.

For me, it felt like another full circle moment, though not exactly a positive one. How strange it was knowing that Ky and I had come from exactly the same environment, but were living such different lives – one of us in prison as an inmate, and the other employed to support inmates to help them stop them reoffending.

There was another poignant moment that struck me hard when I was working in the prison system. I was working with a woman and her adult daughter, both inmates, and both of them in my program. There was such a well of grief and anger between them.

'I feel like I've failed,' the mother told me. 'I didn't want my daughter to end up in here, but I'm the one to blame, aren't I?'

There was so much shame and fear emanating from this woman. All she'd wanted for her daughter was a better life, but she hadn't been able to make that happen. That's the hard thing about the cycles of poverty and addiction – they make it hard, almost impossible sometimes, for people not to reoffend. Sometimes crime is the easier option, and I could see this reflected in my own mother's story, and in Ky's.

Talking to this woman in prison, I realised that Mum might have had similar feelings about Ky's addiction and the time she'd spent in prison. Mum was as much a victim of her addiction and poverty as the rest of us were, and this made me even more determined to use my skills to help these women.

Not too long after this, I found out that Ky had given birth to a baby boy, Adam, once she'd left prison. Now there was another beautiful little boy added to our family. But again, caught as she was in the relentless cycle of substance abuse, mental illness and poverty, Ky wasn't able to be the mother Adam deserved.

Just when we hoped that 2021 would return us all to a pre-pandemic normal, there we were back in the thick of it with the new strain of COVID-19. For the most part, Western Australia managed to avoid the strict lockdowns that were rolled out along the east coast of Australia, and while I was able to continue to work and socialise without too much disruption, I was starting to feel restless again.

I was also juggling more and more work as an Indigenous creative and I knew there'd be more opportunities to explore in Sydney or Melbourne. I started wondering whether it was time for me to try my luck on the other side of the country again.

Then, on Valentine's Day, when there was a brief loosening of border restrictions, I flew to Melbourne for a catch up with a group of amazing First Nations women who all had some kind of public or social media presence. We'd connected online and had realised that we could create a really wonderful and supportive community if we helped and promoted each other in our work. When I was there in Melbourne, I started to picture myself living there. It had been a couple of years since I'd given Sydney a go, and I was older, wiser and more confident now than I had been back then. I also had bigger networks and had made more friends on the east coast since appearing on *The Bachelor* and *Bachelor in Paradise*.

It was hard thinking about leaving Perth again – but it wasn't hard at all thinking about living in Melbourne. I loved the focus on the arts in Melbourne and the really strong, progressive First Nations and LGBTQIA+ communities. I also loved the café culture – and the coffee! – and truth be told, the winter fashions too. As a WA girl, I'd spent my life in shorts and thongs and loved pulling on gorgeous long boots and coats to match the cold weather in Melbourne. I knew if I moved again, I'd miss my family, my friends, and being close to country. It was always difficult living away from Mum's and Nan's resting places, but my recent trip up north had reminded me that family and country were never going to leave me, and living apart from them didn't mean I wouldn't stay connected. I could always drop back home for visits whenever I needed.

So when I went back to Perth, it was to start the process of packing up my home and moving to a new one. I'd already found somewhere to live in Melbourne, and now it was just a matter of waiting out the rest of the time on my lease with Alex, and book flights for Cobar and me to travel to the east coast. As it turned out, it would be for good this time!

I'm always amazed at how easily my life can fit into a few suitcases. Growing up the way I did made me a minimalist; there isn't much else that's important to me that I can't carry in a suitcase in each of my hands.

When I arrived back in Melbourne in March 2021, I was ready for a new beginning. And again, I could never have imagined what was waiting for me just around the corner.

When *The Bachelorette* came knocking, I'd only been living in Melbourne for a few months. Ever since my appearance on *The Bachelor*, I knew my name had been thrown around the mix of potential suitors, but I hadn't seriously thought for a second that I'd end up on television again, this time as the face of the 2021 season. I was so grateful for the connections and the networks I'd made through Bachie, but I knew what a huge toll it took on your life to gamble on finding love under the glare of a national spotlight.

I know there are cynics who might think otherwise, but there is a genuine quest for love at the heart of the *Bachelor* and *Bachelorette* series. Even if you believe that people agree to appear on the programs for exposure or fame and glory, the fact is that any group of humans in close quarters and out of touch with the rest of the world will form close bonds over time – and romance is an inevitable part of that.

Regardless, I knew it would be a huge commitment to join the show as the suitor. As one of the contestants vying for the attention of the suitor, you're only responsible for *your* actions, and your *own* heart. But as the suitor, there are so many people relying on you, and I knew that I wouldn't take anyone's wellbeing, feelings or mental health lightly. I also knew there is a balancing act being played out in reality television, and the result is something that falls somewhere between the truth and the best story. When I appeared on *The Bachelor*, I was naive about the process, and this time, if I accepted the offer, I would need to protect myself, and be very clear about my intentions.

There was a lot to weigh up. In the end, I did what I always do when I need to make a decision – I went outside, into nature, got my body moving and interrogated what I wanted from my life, and whether being the Bachelorette would serve that purpose. I thought a lot about Mum and Nan, and what they would think, and I thought a lot about what it would mean to be the first bisexual, Aboriginal contestant in the history of the show.

The description 'bisexual' has always been tricky for me, because I've never seen my sexuality as being captured by a label. It's such a binary term, and for me, gender isn't a factor when I fall in love, whether it's with a man, with a woman, with a non-binary person ... with whoever. For me, it's always been about the human. If I had to use a term, 'pansexual' is a far better fit.

That said, I'd spent a lot of time dodging expectations from my gay friends that I was a lesbian, and dodging expectations from my straight friends that I was straight. I knew firsthand just how hard it was for people to accept and understand bisexuality for what it is, and I wondered if my appearance on the show would make a difference to others who identified like me. It would be enough of a challenge asking audiences to connect with a so called 'bi' suitor without trying to educate them about gender and sexual diversity at the same time!

I could see clearly that I had a great opportunity to create real awareness and even spark real change by being a representative of the LGBTQIA+ community on mainstream, free-to-air television. There was the same kind of opportunity being an Indigenous suitor on the show. And to me, that felt like a *big* deal.

Since I appeared on the show, there have been various comments made to me that it's important not to overstate or exaggerate the significance of being the first Indigenous Bachelorette – the logic is that it's hardly the same as being the first Indigenous Prime Minister. I understand that perspective, of course – for those who are lucky enough to be able to switch off from national politics or social justice issues, reality television is just light entertainment. But I don't agree with that perspective, because, being Aboriginal, everything in my life *is* political. I am political just by existing.

First Nations people have been stereotyped since invasion, and that means that every time one of us does anything notable – good, bad or indifferent – it's seen as a reflection of *all of us*.

When you oppress a minority, you take away their rights to individuality, and make them into a type because it makes it easier to dehumanise them that way.

For the non-Indigenous people who don't think it's a big deal for a national free-to-air broadcaster to choose a First Nations woman as their Bachelorette, that might be because what they've seen on screen is attainable for them. As Osher would say later in his opening comments on the show, 'You can't be it if you can't see it', never a truer thing has been spoken about representation for First Nations people on commercial television.

I knew that appearing on *The Bachelorette* wasn't going to save lives necessarily, but perhaps if we'd known, when we were growing up as kids in Carnarvon, that being mob was something to be proud of, that we could own our culture and our country on national telly, that we could be whatever we wanted to be, *including* a TV star, perhaps that visibility could have prevented so many of us from dropping out of school, or turning to drugs and alcohol.

Perhaps if I'd seen queer love on television when I was growing up, I would have felt confident enough to own the feelings I felt for the girls I loved, instead of feeling shame and anxiety, which contributed in its own way to the spiral that led to my suicide attempt.

My contribution might only have been one drop in the ocean, but without each and every single drop, how do we ever get to a full wave of change?

I decided to do it. It wasn't a decision made lightly. My heart had healed, and I was ready to open myself up to the possibility of love again. And I was also ready to open that love up to all of Australia, in the hopes that it would create an even bigger love –

love and acceptance for difference and diversity, and everything that I could represent as the first bisexual, Aboriginal *Bachelorette*.

I rang the producers and said yes. And the whirlwind started all over again.

There's a lot I could say about *The Bachelorette*, but really there's no way to describe the intensity, the insanity, the highs and the hardships of taking part in a reality program like this one. For the months that we were filming, it took up one hundred per cent of every waking moment. The crew, the producers and support team became like a family to me, and the contestants took all of my focus.

When I commit to something, I commit fully. I went into the show wanting not only to do my family and my communities proud, but because I was genuinely ready to find love again. Having fallen in love before on television, I knew there was a very high chance of meeting someone special, and I was lucky to meet so many truly amazing people in my season.

Walking onto set as the suitor was a very different dynamic to when I was a contestant. For a start, I was living on my own, in a separate house. I'd requested that because I knew I'd need physical space away from the main residence for the sake of my mental health, and it meant I could take Cobar, my dog, with me. He was such a big part of keeping me sane through the weeks and weeks of filming!

Being the suitor meant that every time I entered a room, whether the cameras were on or off, all eyes were trained on me. And every time, I was aware of the responsibility on my shoulders – every single one of the contestants had given up three months of their lives to meet me.

There were things I absolutely loved about the process – the beautiful clothes, spending time with my friends in the crew, especially my amazing producers Spencer and Maz, and Nat and Dean, and meeting each of the contestants and getting to know them a little more on fun or exciting dates, which might see us painting, or rock climbing, or anything in between. There were some crazy things too, like the kiss that Jamie-Lee and I shared on top of Sydney's tallest building, which at the time smashed the Guinness World Book of Records for the longest onscreen pash!

But there were moments that were really tough, like meeting such incredible people and knowing that I was going to hurt their feelings. I wished I could spend more time with each contestant, to actually give them the attention they deserved. I wasn't part of the casting process, so I really was meeting everyone for the first time once we started filming. I knew there were some who didn't actually care about me, who were chasing fame. And I thought, *You do you*. I couldn't control that.

What I wasn't expecting were the depth of the real friendships and romances that formed. I think my heart is just always open to love, and I knew there was every possibility I really would meet my person during the show.

As much as the finished product looks like a fairytale, the truth is that everything in TV production runs on a really tight schedule, so in reality I was only getting the equivalent of a few minutes at a time with each of the contestants, and it was important for the good conversations to be on camera, so the process of filming was a continual juggling act. I was also very conscious of not holding the crew up beyond their usual filming hours – the last thing I wanted was to be the reason why they'd be late getting home to their kids! The realities of production meant that I had to hustle, and hustle fast, to get to know everyone.

But the biggest thing I had to get used to very quickly was literally being the centre of everyone's attention. Having watched other seasons and suitors over the years, it always seemed to me that they were completely comfortable having all eyes and cameras on them.

But I grew up trying to be invisible. When people looked at me, it hadn't always been a positive thing – security staff thinking I was stealing, people trying to figure out where I was from, and staring when I was with a girlfriend and holding hands. To come from the margins and take up the spotlight felt intimidating at times, and something that niggled about taking up that spotlight was that if I screwed up, there was every possibility that audiences would blame it on my cultural background or my communities. That's Tokenism 101: there are so few blak, bi women on TV – if there's one of us with a public profile, we carry the responsibility of representing everyone, which is as bad as it can be good.

I also had to make a big adjustment from being a completely independent person and captain of my own ship to being watched like a hawk. Even something as simple as needing to go to the toilet required breaks in filming and an OK from the team. I probably had a few 'diva' moments when it came to situations like these, especially with the early starts and long nights of filming. If I didn't have my coffee in the morning, it wasn't pretty! More than once I thanked God I had Cobar to keep me grounded.

There were some really moving and important things we introduced into my season of *The Bachelorette*, which I'm still so proud of today. One of them was in the first episode, a proper Welcome to Country ceremony – I cried happy tears as Uncle Colin Locke welcomed us to the country of the Darug nation alongside Uncle Peter Williams and Uncle Wayne Cornish. I was so moved. When that episode aired I received such an avalanche of joy and pride from mob, and so many other friends and fans who could see what a significant moment it was for the representation of First Nations culture on commercial television.

It had all been made possible by Eliza, the First Nations consultant on the show – Eliza's work and presence made me feel so much at home; she ensured that the set was a safe cultural space for me as an Indigenous person, arranging for all the houses on the property to be smoked, including mine, and the mansion where the contestants were staying, and the production team's. She and other diversity and inclusion consultants that Network Ten had hired for the show also made sure that everyone used culturally appropriate and LGBTQIA+ positive language, and Eliza gave me some beautiful weavings and art to hang in my residence to make me feel more at home.

The other was when my friend and sister Amy Thunig came onto the set to meet Darvid and Jamie-Lee and find out what they understood of my Indigenous culture and background. Amy is a Gomeroi woman and academic who I met online during the COVID lockdowns, when I initiated a social media exercise, 30 Days of Deadly Connection, designed to connect First Nations people with each other when we all felt isolated, and promote thirty inspiring First Nations cultural leaders, who I chatted with, one for each day of that month. Amy and I clicked straight away, and I loved having her on the set of *The Bachelorette* because she has such a staunch energy, and watching her grill Darvid and Jamie-Lee about their First Nations cultural awareness and talk about the importance of country, connection to culture and Indigenous history was something I'll never forget.

There were other wonderful things that happened on the show, including the fact that I fell in love. As time and history has shown, it didn't work out to be the fairytale I'd hoped for, but for the whole time I was filming the show, and for the months immediately after, I was completely in love, and it was beautiful. I know that for my season of *The Bachelorette* I gave myself to love with everything I had in me, and I'll always remember and cherish that.

Unfortunately, what could have been the best months of my life became the worst.

On the final day of filming for *The Bachelorette*, when I was saying my goodbyes to the man I had fallen in love with and who I wouldn't see for several months until the show finished airing, back at home in Perth, my sister was dying.

I wouldn't find out until a few days later, when I received a phone call from the Office of the Public Trustee.

As soon as filming for Bachie had wrapped, I checked into an Airbnb in Sydney, where I'd stay before heading back to Melbourne. I was absolutely exhausted. The adrenaline of filming wears off as soon as you're off set, and I was just beginning to process how tired I was after such a full-on few months. Finally, I was alone, and in the quiet my thoughts were running free. I had so much on my mind – I was giddy with love, I was nervous about how the season would come across when it aired in a few months, and I was excited about getting back to my new life in Melbourne and finding a new normal.

Rolling COVID restrictions meant that I hadn't been back to Western Australia to see my family in a while, and I was hoping the borders would open again soon. I missed my siblings, and I missed being on country. It all nagged away at me in the back of mind like a steady tattoo.

As I lay there on the couch my phone rang – it was a call from a blocked number. Normally I don't answer those calls, so I let it go to voicemail, but then it rang again immediately.

I answered it.

'Am I speaking to Brooke Blurton?' the male voice in my ear asked.

'Yes, that's me,' I said.

'I'm calling from the Office of the Public Trustee.'

I knew what he was going to say before he said the words. I sat up, feeling suddenly woozy. You know that sensation when your blood pressure drops suddenly, and you feel as if a breeze could just blow you away? It felt as if the only thing anchoring me to the couch was the phone in my hand, heavy now, and pressed hard to my ear.

'I'm afraid I'm calling to inform you that your sister Kyandra was found dead three days ago, from a suspected overdose.'

He kept talking, and I was reeling. The next few hours were horrific.

The Trustee had apparently been trying to reach me for days, even though I'd had no missed calls or messages. Ky's body was waiting in the morgue in Perth, and I was stuck in Sydney, with borders still shut and a potential two-week wait in quarantine, even if I was allowed back into the state in the first place. Even while my body was shaking from grief, my brain went straight to logistics.

Here's what I know now about how my sister died, pieced together from CCTV footage and information from a security guard.

Ky was found lying down in Yagan Square in Perth by a security guard, quite clearly high and out of it. He tried to help her up, but she told him to get lost. The CCTV footage showed them talking, and then him walking away. The guard returned to check on Ky multiple times through the night, and the last time he checked on her, she wasn't breathing. He called for an ambulance and performed CPR for twenty minutes, until the paramedics arrived and they took over. After another hour, she was pronounced dead. There were needles and empty bottles of alcohol around her.

The fact that I was finishing the filming of a season of one of the biggest reality TV franchises in Australia, and my sister was dying, homeless and alone in Yagan Square, in the middle of a busy city, was devastating. Months later, at the edge of that very precinct, there would be a huge billboard looming over the space, advertising my season of *The Bachelorette*. To add to the heartbreak, Yagan Square is a place of cultural significance for Noongar people, and the statue that is the focal point of the square is an ode to wirin, which is best described as a sacred force that links mother nature to every living creature.

When I hung up, I called Troy straight away. He could tell from my voice that something was wrong.

'It's Ky, isn't it?' he said. Both of us had the same premonition, as if we'd always known it was coming.

I called Eden, told RJ. Each time, my grief washed over me again.

I called my executive producer, Spencer, who had become a close friend, and who lived in Sydney. She dropped everything to come and pick me up, and the next few days staying with her were a total blur as we phoned everyone from government agencies, trying get a permit for me to travel home, to airlines, to other members of my family and mob to let them know what had happened.

I knew the responsibility of organising Ky's funeral would be mine, so I started thinking about what needed to be done – which casket to buy, which flowers Ky would have wanted, which church for the memorial service. At the same time, I was tracking down where Ky's son, Adam, was; that he was safe and in foster care, that his foster parents knew who I was, and had my details.

I had to be practical and organised, but all I wanted to do was curl up and weep. I'd lost all the women in my immediate family now. I was the last one standing.

It was a struggle to get a permit for me to travel back into Western Australia. But the team from *The Bachelorette* understood how important it was for me to be back home, and with their help, including Eliza, the First Nations consultant for the show, we were able to pinpoint a clause in WA's border restriction policies that would allow me to travel home to attend sorry business for Ky. I was so grateful for their kindness and support, and of all my friends who rallied around to help me in those desperate days.

Once I was back in Perth, before I could do anything else, I had to quarantine myself for a fortnight. Police would come and check on me at my Airbnb, to make sure I was complying with the rules. One officer recognised me as the Bachelorette, and snapped a selfie through the gate. It was surreal.

Being back on country felt somewhat grounding, but those two weeks being locked away were agony; I was painfully aware of how long my sister had been gone for and all my energy went into organising the funeral in detail. But finally I was free and I could see my family, and we could put Ky to rest.

In her last two years, Ky's life had been hard. After being released from prison, all accounts suggest that she deteriorated quickly. Without medication, she would have been very ill with schizophrenia, and soon she was back on drugs and wandering the streets looking for money, hoping to score a hit. Her baby Adam was taken away, and put into foster care, which would have been devastating for her.

It's hard for me to know that, for a lot of people, my sister will be remembered as a junkie who lost her kids, who overdosed and died in a public place. She was so much more than her circumstances, but that was all anyone could see of her by the end.

I remember her for who she really was: a sweet, gentle and funny woman. She had the sort of smile that took over her whole face. She looked a lot like our mum. They were like twins. Eden and Ky had the hardest time growing up with Mum, because their childhoods were more defined by her addiction than the rest of us. Ky fell prey to drugs early because there was no one to look out for her, Mum especially. But Ky's addiction and her mental illness weren't what defined her – as well as kindness, she had talent, and I'll always remember that Ky was once been an emerging golf star. But the addiction and mental illness made it hard for her to make good choices; they dictated her life, and she never had the chance to flourish.

If I could have done anything for Ky, I wish I could have been the older, wiser sister, been able to give her a safe landing place.

Somewhere she could be herself, to come and crash whenever she needed. I wish I could have taken her home, and cleaned her up, and put her to bed surrounded with softness and warmth. I wish I could have helped her detox from her drug use, helped her stay on the medication that helped her so much.

There hasn't been a day since Ky died that I haven't thought of her. My brothers and I are closer than ever now. Losing Ky has made us appreciate how much we need each other. In the months following her funeral, I spent a lot of time thinking about our relationship, and how, with just a few twists of fate or chance, her life might have been different. If someone had intervened for Ky, supported her to stay in school, encouraged her to have bigger dreams ... Who knows? She could still be alive now, with both her children in her care, telling her own story.

Then I think about how easily I could have fallen down a similar path if one or two other things had been different in my life. If I hadn't witnessed what teen pregnancy did to my sister, and to Mum, and to Nan before her. If Dad hadn't come to pick me up after Mum's wake. If Leanne hadn't been able to take me in and make me part of her little family. If Jo hadn't taken me in when I was homeless.

It breaks my heart to think like this, but it also sparks something inside me, and makes me even more determined to take every opportunity I have because now I'm living for three angels – Mum, Nan and Ky, three women who deserved more, and who I want to honour in my own life.

I've spent a lot of time thinking about Ky's son, Adam. He's still in foster care, and I stay in touch with his carers, and I know that he's well and surrounded by love. I am deeply committed to being in Adam's life, and I will always be here for him, no matter what. I want to be part of his life while he grows up, and to pass down the cultural knowledge, the family history, and the memories of his mum that I hold inside me. I want Adam to know the good things about his mum, and that she was so much more than the drugs that dictated her life.

I loved my big sister deeply. I know that she's joined Mum and Nan, and that all three are connected to me forever, because death can't take away our bond. Their spirits are with me in everything I do.

Telling my story has been so important for me. I want people to know the truth of my circumstances. They were hard, and a lot of it is shocking, but I also want people to know that for my entire life, love has been the guiding force, and it is still the biggest motivator in my life today.

Where I came from, people don't always have big dreams. Dreams can feel like a luxury, when you're struggling to survive. When I was a kid, I didn't spend my time wishing I was famous, or a TV star. I wished for food, I wished I lived in a normal house, I wished Mum would stay off the drugs. I wished that Nan would live forever. I wished that I could live with my brothers and sister.

Even when Mum and Nan passed and our worlds fell apart, my wishes were full of love. I wished all the time that one day we could be a family again. I dreamed of having a house one day, on country, where family was always welcome, where everyone could come and know they had a safe place to rest.

My wishes and my dreams have always been driven by the love I have for my family, and for my culture, communities, country. Sometimes, they've been driven by the love I have for an individual, and I think you know by now, that when I love someone, I love them deeply and completely. Despite all the heartache I've experienced, it's this capacity for love that has made me who I am.

From the moment I took my first breath, there was love guiding me.

My nan's love for me was fierce, and I could feel it in every moment I spent with her. That woman, so strong and staunch, carried on the traditions of our mob by passing on what she could to her grandchildren about our culture, and about country. Nan showed me love could be big even when it seemed small — a cup of tea with a bickie to dunk in it; watching the footy on television; an art activity she'd painstakingly planned so Troy and I would have a few hours of a normal childhood; lying in bed with her at night, hearing her stories and feeling like nothing bad could ever happen to us for as long as she was with us. Nan was a true matriarch, and I think she passed that torch to me when she died. I am determined to never let that flame die.

Mum wasn't always able to show the love she had for us, but I never once doubted it. Every single one of her children inherited Mum's big, wild heart. She was untamable, and she lived big and hard — and like the brightest lights, she didn't shine for long enough. I love Mum without question, because even on the worst day of my life, when she left us, I never once questioned that she loved us.

My brothers and I, the last left of our immediate family, will always hold onto each other. It's hard for me being so far away from them on the other side of the country, but our love doesn't need proximity to thrive. I think of Eden, Troy and RJ every single day and talk to them most days, too. They are the grounding force in my crazy life, my reminder of home and of my purpose.

My family is in my blood, but I wouldn't have come this far without the love of those who chose me as family, even when they didn't have to.

Leanne, Jo, Pete – they each owed me nothing, and yet they gave me everything. I'm so incredibly grateful for them, and I learned something incredibly valuable from each, and that is that the greatest opportunities in life are often in lifting someone else up. If they hadn't reached out their hands to me when they did, I wouldn't be here today. I'm determined to pay that forward in my life.

There are so many other people who changed the course of my life, as well as entire communities that have changed me irrevocably. I don't know what my life would have been without footy, and the girls I met playing it.

In many ways, footy saved my life. For so many years, it was the one consistent anchor in the chaos. I loved the joy and sense of release that came with the physicality of it, but even more, I loved the people. The women I played footy with gave me a safe environment to explore and unpack my sexuality, they lifted me out of my worst depressions, and gave me a boot in the arse when I needed it, too! They taught me about giving everything to achieve a shared goal, and about pushing past my limits, striving for more, and never giving up.

Despite all the hardship, I have been so rich in love.

People like to remind me that I am very young, but I feel like an old soul. I'm tied to this country through my blood, and to my communities by choice. I know I'm only at start of my journey, but if I keep love at the centre of everything I do, only good things can come.

When Ky died, I was on the brink of a new beginning and it reminded me that no matter what happens in life, our roots never change. I might have networks now that I could never have imagined before, but the ones that really matter to me are the same ones I was born with. My blood networks. My mob. My connection to country. Those are parts of me that will never, ever change. And my ability to love – I'll never lose that.

One of the greatest gifts that my experience as the Bachelorette gave me was the community I found online. It was overwhelming to hear from so many young people across Australia who had been grappling with their own sexuality, and to hear how important it was for them to see me showing the depth and capacity of queer relationships.

To see sexual diversity on TV, not as a gimmick but as a genuine display of love, has been important for so many people, and it's humbling to know that I helped bring that to Australian audiences. Similarly, hearing from mob that my role on TV gave them a sense of pride is so gratifying.

To me, this is the definition of big love. Love that is more than an individual or a couple, more than a moment in time, or a single narrative. For me, big love is about reclaiming my identity from all the trauma and baggage of my past, and owning how those experiences have shaped me, without letting them own me.

It's about reclaiming my heritage, my culture and my country as a source of strength and spirit, instead of the stereotypes and racism that I grew up with.

Big love is about community, and about sharing our strength and our purpose with each other. It's about using that strength and purpose to help and support each other, and to inspire each other about what's possible, and that's what I try to do every single day.

It's never been easy. There will always be people trying to define me, to put me a nice, neat box and tell me who I am. But if my story can tell you one thing, it's that I am a fighter. A tough little tacker, as Nan would have said.

I have been through so much to get to where I am.

And the best thing is, I'm only getting started.

Epilogue

Dear little one,

I can picture you so clearly — at age eleven, you are already on your way to becoming a fierce young woman.

I am proud of you. But I am also scared for you, because I know that there's so much to come in the next few years, so much sadness and hardship that I wish I could shelter you from.

But, Brooke, the thing about life is that it's the hard things that create the strength in you. It's the hard things will see you through to the beautiful, amazing future I know is in store.

I want you to know that, even though it might not always feel like it, everything will be OK. In a way, I think you already know that. You have an intuition that is beyond your years, one you've inherited from Mum and from Nan. It's part of you, the way country and culture are part of you. No one can take it away, and it will guide you at all times.

Your whole life, you've watched and analysed people, their behaviour, how they interact with one another, and you've seen what can make someone and what can break someone. You've seen people reach their limits, and you've come to learn your own. But more importantly, you've discovered the well of strength inside you, and I can promise you that it will overflow when you need it the most.

I know that there's a part of you, a secret certainty you have, that you are meant for bigger things in life. Sometimes you feel ashamed of this feeling, as if it makes you arrogant or stuck up. But you only feel that way because the world has told you so many times that you aren't special – you've experienced racism, violence, loss and poverty. You have been pushed down and beaten by life, but you just keep getting up again.

I want you to know, Brooke, that the inner voice you have that says you're worthy of more is right. You *are* worthy of more. You *are* meant for bigger things. You are so much more than your circumstances, Brooke, and you're going to prove that to everyone.

Before light there's always darkness, and I'm sorry to say that there is still more pain and loss you have to get through before you reach that light. But there's a lot that you're going to gain, which you can't even imagine yet.

You are going to have moments of such intense joy, you'll feel like you're going to burst. You're going to meet people who prove to you that humans are capable of so much good, people who give you safety and sanctuary and love when you need it the most. You're going to climb mountains that feel insurmountable, and when you reach their peak – because you will – you'll see views you can't begin to imagine. You're going to find resilience that you never knew you had, because even though you've experienced more hardship in your short life than most people will ever experience, you're tough. You're scrappy, and strong, and you never quit, Brooke. Believe in yourself.

Your biggest asset is your heart. You have a capacity for love that will be the driving force in your life. It draws people to you, and keeps the special ones close. Love is everything, Brooke. Don't forget that.

But at the same time, don't worry so much about it. Don't worry about who's going to love you, or how they're going to love you, or when you're going to find love. I know it might seem hard to believe right now, but when love is right, it will feel easy. It isn't meant to be hard.

Most importantly, you'll recognise love when you see it.

Love is the most infinite and effortless presence in this world. It's found in the tiny crevices of human nature. It's not all grand gestures, and moonlight cruises, and song and fanfare. Love is in the little things, in the ordinary parts of our extraordinary lives. It's found in hospital rooms, and grocery stores, in home-cooked meals and in the smiles of passing strangers.

Love is in the music you listen to, and in the jokes you make, and it's in the way a part of you is always living on country, and how country will always be waiting to welcome you when you return.

Love is 'Are you OK?' and 'Get home safe' and 'Did you have enough to eat?' It's in the feeling of being completely at ease with someone, because being happy just feels normal after a while. The best kind of boring – the feeling of security when you are loved unconditionally.

Little one, you don't need to worry about love. It's all around you, every day, in every moment. It can reach you at your best and it will meet you at your worst. There's no force in the world stronger than love. BIG LOVE.

There's no reason to believe that love can't find you. Because you already have it in you.

Brooke, there are going to be times when you think about giving up. I wish so much that I could reach back into time to tell you that these moments of darkness are just that – brief moments in time, which will pass.

Don't give in when you hear those voices that tell you you're not enough. You *are* enough. You are so much more than the worst moments you have. You have a purpose in life, Brooke, and you're going to find that sooner than you think.

The path you're on might not always make sense, but trust me when I tell you that everything happens for a reason. (You're going to say that a lot, by the way, but it is one hundred per cent true.) No matter how strange it may feel, every step you take now is leading you to exactly where you need to be.

I've seen your destination, and it is beautiful, Brooke.

Take your time on the journey. Go into it with clear eyes and an open heart.

There is so much waiting for you.

Love,
Brooke

Acknowledgements

Big Love is a message of hope and love for anyone who's ever felt like they didn't belong in this world.

I want to thank those who have helped me bring *Big Love* to light, and give big love to those who made my dream come true.

First, I want to thank Zoya Patel for her time, patience and help in the truth-telling of my story. Thanks to my publisher, Roberta Ivers, and the entire HarperCollins team for helping me believe that my story was worth telling, with extra thanks to the hardworking sales team. Thanks to designer Mietta Yans for my beautiful book cover, and to photographer Jarrad Seng for his brilliant photography.

Thanks to my management, Genevieve Day of Day Management, and Andre Bognar and Sarah Wagner from The Society Agency for all their support and encouragement.

Huge thanks to my beautiful siblings, who have been by my side for the entire ride, and have shaped me into the person I am, so that I've been able to tell not only my story, but our family's story.

Finally, thanks to every single person who came into my life and gave me big love.

Resources

If you need someone to talk to, or want to find out more, these organisations can help you. Many have specific support for people who are LGBTQIA+.

Head to Health
www.headtohealth.gov.au
A guide to digital mental health services from some of Australia's most trusted mental health organisations

Qlife
www.qlife.org.au
Counselling and referral service for LGBTQIA+ people,
call 1800 184 527 or chat online

Beyond Blue
www.beyondblue.org.au
For anyone feeling depressed or anxious,
call 1300 22 4636 or chat online

Headspace
www.headspace.org.au
Mental health service for ages 12–25

ReachOut.com
www.au.reachout.com
Youth mental health service, visit the website for info
or use the online forum

Lifeline
www.lifeline.org.au
Support for anyone having a personal crisis,
call 13 11 14 or chat online

Suicide Call Back Service
www.suicidecallbackservice.org.au
For anyone thinking about suicide, call 1300 659 467

Kids Helpline
www.kidshelpline.com.au
Help for young people aged 5–25,
call 1800 55 1800

1800Respect
www.1800respect.org.au
National and domestic family and sexual violence counselling service,
call 1800 737 732

13Yarn
www.13yarn.org.au
Aboriginal and Torres Strait Islander support,
call 13 92 76

Minus18
www.minus18.org.au
LGBTQIA+ youth support

You may also be interested in visiting these sites:

ACON
www.acon.org.au
For LGBTQIA+ health and HIV prevention and support

PFLAG
www.pflagaustralia.org.au
For parents, family and friends of lesbians and gays